TAROT
PREDICTIONS
2019

Karmel Nair was born Catholic, is married to a Hindu, and practises the Buddhist way of life. She worked in a media house and was a successful radio jockey with leading radio stations before she embarked on a career in tarot fortune-telling. Karmel discovered her intuitive powers as she delved deeper into the tarot world. Tarot led her to the most magnificent discovery of her life – Vipassana, the study and practice of mindfulness.

This book, Karmel's fifth, is a product of her experience in learning and understanding tarot and human nature. *Tarot Predictions 2019* is not only a book about the future, it is also a medium of changing the future through spiritual realization by harnessing the power of the being within us.

Karmel is now a certified life coach, who uses her skills of scientific coaching to help people achieve the most from their life.

She can be reached at karmel@tarotreader.in or coach@karmelnair.com.

TAROT PREDICTIONS 2019

KARMEL NAIR

HarperCollins *Publishers* India

First published in India by
HarperCollins *Publishers* in 2018
A-75, Sector 57, Noida, Uttar Pradesh 201301, India
www.harpercollins.co.in

2 4 6 8 10 9 7 5 3 1

P-ISBN: 978-93-5302-012-5
E-ISBN: 978-93-5302-013-2

Typeset in 10/12.5 Adobe Caslon Pro at
Manipal Digital Systems, Manipal

Printed and bound at
Thomson Press (India) Ltd.

'Om mani padme hum'

'With constant practice of mindfulness you can transform the impure body, speech and mind into the pure body, speech and mind of a Buddha.'

– Anonymous

Contents

Note to the Readers

In this section, I will discuss the importance of living in the moment, mindfulness and the adverse effects of mindlessness. I have discussed anicca (impermanence) and apranahita (aimlessness) in previous books, and will discuss another interesting theory associated with mindfulness here – the concept of 'no mind'.

WHAT IS NO MIND?

The concept of no mind is described thus in the film *The Last Samurai*: It is the basis of creation, the basis of life of the samurais. The film discusses how being in no mind can help you achieve what you desire and can even help in attaining salvation. Later, I read up on this concept and discovered that no mind means the space in your mind where your mind doesn't exist, where your mind is empty. This is the part of the mind which does not have ego or emotions of anger, desire, fear, love or hate. Can you imagine a time, even for a second, when you are free from the constant chattering in your mind? I am sure you have never experienced this state. But if you do think about this concept and do the work required, you may be able to glimpse the no mind zone.

Whenever I can't sleep, I find I can hear my thoughts of fear, insecurity, pain and misery so loudly that they bother me. At times like this, I usually give up on trying to sleep and give in to my chattering mind, which makes me a slave to it. You may be doing this too, when you are restless and unable to sleep. The mind is a formidable opponent; it is hard to defeat and will not go down without a fight.

The only way to train your mind to listen and submit to you is to create empty spaces in it; in other words, create a no mind zone. No mind is the state when thoughts don't exist, when you are open to everything, unlike in the normal state when your mind tends to latch on to thoughts and manipulates them. Let's try to understand how your mind behaves normally by looking at the example below:

Imagine you get a call from your boss and he tells you, 'Hey listen, I want to talk to you about something important. It's not great news and I hope you take it well. Let me know when you are here and we can chat.'

While you are listening to this conversation, you may start having horrific thoughts such as: 'Chat means what? Am I going to be fired? Oh God, yes I am going to be fired! No job means no money, I will default on my mortgage payment. I can't buy the car now. How will I pay my bills? My kid's school fees are not going to be paid. Oh God, I am doomed, I am a loser. What do I tell my wife/husband? What do I tell my friends? I am no good, I am just a pathetic living creature. I will never find a job in time, it will take me a year to find a job that pays me this much. I am useless. I don't like this man who just fired me, he needs to be out of this place and not me. I am dead meat, I am doomed.'

These thoughts of anger, dejection and disappointment are all symptoms of a state which is the opposite of no mind. Observe how your mind drove you to assume what your boss was planning to say to you. You jumped to conclusions and became stressed and worried without a legitimate reason. You have no idea what your boss is going to discuss with you but your mind has led you to focus on the worst-case scenario. If you have had thoughts of this kind in other situations, then you know how you are enslaved to your mind and its incessant chattering.

Now if you were in the no mind zone, you are likely to have handled the comment from your boss in the following way:

You will be fully present in the moment while listening to your boss talking. You will be devoid of any prejudice, anger, resentment or thought. You will simply be listening. At the end of the call, you will smile with amusement, wondering what your boss wants to discuss. You won't dissect the information he provided, and neither will you judge it as good or bad. What the discussion will be about or what its outcome will be doesn't concern you at all. You will put the phone down and resume what you were doing – perhaps washing the dishes – before the call.

You will resume doing the dishes mindfully, feel the water on your fingers and the foam of the liquid soap, and focus on rinsing them. You will do this task with your full attention, without any other thought. Neither will you reflect on the call you just received. You will simply be in the no mind zone in which you are not attached to any thoughts, disturbed by negative ideas or joyous because of positive thoughts. You are focused only on doing the dishes. This is how your mind will appear when you are in a state of no mind; when the mind is quiet, calm and focused on the task assigned to it.

BENEFITS OF THE STATE OF NO MIND

You will benefit greatly when you reach the state of no mind, even if it is for a second. Imagine a minute of no thought, no tension, no worries, no pain and no fear. An empty mind! In such a state, you can achieve eternal happiness. Unfortunately, the only people who seem to practise no mind are the monks. They practise no mind all day long. If you speak to them, you will realize how detached they are from worldly desires, which makes them calm and peaceful.

You can begin practising no mind by taking small steps. Through this practice, you will achieve moments of bliss and learn to calmly handle the stress in your life. No mind teaches you to approach concepts in a detached manner, without any inhibitions and illusions. You simply look at everything from the perspective of a third person and are not affected by situations, problems or difficulties. You become the watcher, the observer who sees emotion without identifying with it.

When you begin to observe your thoughts, you begin to exert control over your mind. You begin to drive your thoughts from negative standpoints to positive ones. You begin to control your emotions. Whether you are feeling happy or sad, you will be aware of what is happening inside you. This gives you power over your mind. The next time you are in a difficult situation, start observing the mindless chatter in your mind and simply smile at it. As you begin to observe the noise in your head in a detached manner, your negative or positive emotions will disappear.

You could be involved in a situation where someone is screaming or pointing fingers at you. If you are in a state of no mind, you will begin to look at this person as someone who is cursing your ego and trying to attack your mind. You will look at this person as someone who is wounded and needs to vent to feel better. You will begin to feel good that you could help this person because he or she could vent to you. You will begin to detach from your ego and, therefore, your mind.

Your mind will have control over you as long as your ego is involved. The moment the ego and 'I, me and myself' disappear from your identity, your mind will no longer have power over you. You will then achieve a state of no mind and you will simply be in the present moment, where fears and inhibitions don't matter, good and bad don't have any importance, and neither does wealth. You become enlightened, and the realization that you have power over your mind becomes your greatest tool to achieve success.

If you start watching your thoughts and not identifying with them, you will achieve the following benefits:

- ❖ You will have control over both anger and ego.
- ❖ Love, hatred, pain, misery and other emotions will have no impact on you.
- ❖ You will handle situations calmly and practically.
- ❖ You will have greater clarity and your purpose will begin to surface.
- ❖ You will see beyond 'I, me and myself'.
- ❖ You will be separated from yourself. You will become the watcher and will no longer be the thinker.
- ❖ You will be able to positively align every emotion, thought and idea; which will help you achieve success, material gain and emotional stability.

The no mind technique is highly experiential and its experience will vary from person to person. What I gain from it may be different from what you gain from it. You can judge its potential only after you begin to attain this state.

HOW TO ACHIEVE THE STATE OF NO MIND

You cannot achieve a no mind state overnight. It takes years and years of steady practice. Even after decades of practice, holy men may only attain glimpses of the state. Therefore, instead of attaining nirvana your focus should be on attaining a calm and composed demeanour so that you have positive thoughts and are able to channelize your energy into achieving happy outcomes. Everyone wants to be happy: new cars, a big home, a fat pay cheque, a hefty bank balance are all aimed at enhancing happiness. You should know happiness is actually a state of mind. It is the result of no mind.

Observe every thought that comes to your mind and notice your emotions

This is easier said than done. Your first reaction to any situation will be to identify with the situation and immediately get carried away by the chatter of the mind. Well, this is the challenge: the moment such nonsensical blabbering begins in your head, stop and watch it like an external observer. If you do this often you will begin to realize that when you observe a thought or a feeling, it loses its power over you. The more you tune in to your thoughts and feelings, the more easily you begin to detach yourself from them.

Meditate while walking, washing or driving

Who says that meditation can only be done while you are sitting still? Instead of practising sitting meditation, which is tough to do initially, you can practise something that comes more naturally to you, e.g. walking meditation.

You can do this when you are out for your daily walk: Watch every step you take. Observe how one leg goes up and the other stays down. Feel the pressure when your feet touch the ground.

Count each step you take and name them left down, right down, etc. This way you will be mindful while walking, and will prevent your mind from wandering. If your mind does wander to the past or the future, gently bring it back to the present and begin counting each step again.

You can even try this approach while you are driving or washing dishes. Every time you are at the wheel, name every activity you perform while driving, such as accelerating, braking, etc. When your mind wanders, name it and gently bring it back to where it should be. Similarly, name what you do while washing dishes. This way your mind will gradually come under your control and you will know when it wanders.

EXPERIENCE THE STATE OF NO MIND

After continuous practice of being the observer, you will begin to experience empty spaces. This may happen any time; for instance, while you are having a cup of coffee. You may have no other thought in your mind at this time, except for the enjoyment of coffee. You will be able to smell its aroma, taste its rich flavour and hear the gulping sound when you sip it. This is when you will begin to notice the calm state of your mind, which is no mind.

This state of mindfulness may not last longer than the time you take to drink the cup of coffee but it will show you what true happiness feels like. You may also experience this state of no mind when you are listening to a pleasant song. As you begin to enjoy this state of no mind, you will try to achieve it more often.

Aries – Emperor
21 March–19 April

♈

Aries in tarot is described by the Emperor card. It is the first of the zodiac signs and has the natural ability to lead, hence the tarot trump Emperor rightly associates with its qualities. The Emperor leads by example, by power and by dominion. These are your instincts as an Arian, a king in every aspect. Attitude, charisma, intellect and leadership skills come naturally to you, but so do arrogance, insecurity and self-centredness. These qualities are two sides of the same coin.

Aries has a peculiar trait of childish stubbornness and overpowering zest. If you compare the qualities you as an Aries exhibit with those of an Emperor, you will realize that there is a remarkable similarity between the two. You are authoritative, childishly stubborn and easily influenced. You have a natural knack for being a good leader and you are patient and sensitive, which makes you an emotional individual. Now let's compare these qualities with those of an Emperor. An Emperor is strong-headed and focused. He is authoritative and easily influenced by factors such as the urge for conquests, hunger for wealth and the unrelenting desire for power. On the flip side, the Emperor is also childish when it comes to his overbearing emotions. Sometimes this could make him sensitive towards the needs of his people, thus making him a good leader or, conversely, it could make his emotions overpowering enough to force people to succumb to his demands. You are described in tarot with the Emperor card as it perfectly fits in with your qualities in every aspect – your personality, mental strength and your spiritual inclination.

The Emperor card from the Rider-Waite tarot has a king seated on a majestic throne wearing a red robe. The throne is the symbol of power and authority; his robe, red against the card's orange background, stands for the fire and earth elements in amalgamation. Fire denotes aggression and fiery stubbornness, while earth stands for stability, poise and calm temperament. The staff in his right hand symbolizes authority and dominion, and his crown stands for experience and wisdom. The colour of his robe stands for courage, valour and aggression to take on new challenges. The ram's head on the throne, also the sign of Aries, denotes enthusiasm and vigour. The card is numbered four, as in the fourth month of the year, i.e., April, the month of Aries. Four is considered a masculine number, true to its association with the Emperor card in tarot. It is a divine number, a number that denotes the right balance between law, order and fairness. The Emperor denotes both the Aries man and woman. It classically symbolizes the head of the family, a dominating spouse, a temperamental and fair boss or an enthusiastic lover who is perceived as the more mature one in the relationship. As the head of the family, you are the provider, gentle and kind, a good mentor for your children and a rule-setter for the family. This is your emotional and sensitive side at its best. You will see to it that the laws are obeyed and question when they are not. The Emperor is the perfect example of courage and valour, which is why you are often ready to plunge into challenges. You stand up for your own decisions, good or bad. As a boss, the Emperor is the perfect leader; authority, stability, dependability and equality are the ruling attributes of this card.

The Emperor has negative traits too. You are demanding, aggressive and hot-headed, which could cause problems in the upbringing and exert the wrong kind of influence on family members. As a spouse, the Emperor is the dominant one, constantly wanting to prove his point and therefore, most often, imposing it on the other. Your authority and enthusiasm make you very attractive to the opposite sex, but at times you can be unnecessarily possessive and dominating, making the relationship lopsided. As a difficult boss, you can be a tyrant, over-demanding and assertive, making life difficult for your subordinates. You can be the don't-mess-with-me kind.

Spirituality doesn't come naturally to the Emperor. He is a master sign of ego and power, the two qualities that take him away from spirituality. To walk the path of spirituality, you will have to shed the Emperor's skin, forsake your power and ego, which, in all honesty, I see as a rare possibility. The Emperor's only saviour here is his need to help his people; this alone can liberate him. Likewise, you may choose spirituality only if there ever arises a feeling to serve mankind, an urge to reach out to others and end the suffering. This could be the only reason why you would ever abandon your throne and kingship, and choose to follow the path of spirituality. However, knowing the emperor's strong will, he is quite capable of doing this. I hope you have enjoyed knowing yourself through tarot.

This book will take you through the future through five different aspects: Monthly predictions, Love, Health, Wealth and Career.

MONTHLY PREDICTIONS

JANUARY

A situation will unfold this month where you may feel defeated and helpless. There is very little you can do to change this except going along with it. Don't fight it out, instead, take this defeat in the right spirit and you will get an opportunity to fight back in due course. While you are battling this upheaval, situations on the personal front look quite positive. Your family life will be filled with happiness and joy.

FEBRUARY

A good news is on its way. This news pertains to wealth and health. February is a month of abundance and indulgence. I see you making enough to save and spend on yourself. You will be seen pampering yourself and indulging in all the joys money can buy.

MARCH

Stiff competition awaits you this month. If you are seeking a job or an assignment, know that there are formidable opponents seeking the same. Your chances are good, provided you play fair. There is an element of love in your life this month. You will be attracted to an endearing and warm character. A woman will play an important role in your life. Your love life will keep you actively involved all through March.

APRIL

You shall accomplish an impossible task this month. Something comes to completion and it was something you dearly desired. This will bring forth joy and happiness. The odds at work may not look that good. You may find yourself in a spot where work is tight, and the pressure will continue to mount. All you need to do is hang in there and be patient and the situation will gradually settle down.

MAY

You may be stuck between two difficult choices, each pulling you in the opposite direction. The battle between the two would have to end soon if you want some peace. The sooner you choose one and move on, the earlier you will find solace. You may grow impatient regarding some financial gains that seem to be stuck. The money will come along when it is time. You need to be patient and positive.

JUNE

Something somewhere is not all that right and this revelation shall leave you heartbroken. Promises could be broken and people may turn away from their word. Don't let this break you down, there is progress this month and you will continue to move on. You may undertake extensive air travel and capitalize on opportunities life throws at you in the form of networking windows.

JULY

You shall receive good news this month. The news pertains to matters of the heart. You are ready to initiate steps in your love life. Although the news brings a window of opportunity, it also brings confusion and dilemma. You may find yourself in a predicament that seems difficult to resolve. Take your time and think it through; you shall reach a decision soon but do adopt caution.

AUGUST

You will be in a fix where you seem to be losing interest in either your love life or any other such important aspect of life. Instead of blaming others, tarot advises you to look within. You may just find the answers to your questions if you are willing to accept your share of the blame. There is a silver lining in everything and so does it apply to your life. Recovery is certain if you continue to have a strong heart, and work around the difficulties with patience and consistency.

SEPTEMBER

A partnership will be initiated this month. This partnership pertains to work or love. You will get together with someone important and interesting to initiate a new beginning. This joint venture or partnership looks promising, provided both parties exert their will. However, do avoid adopting a negative wealth mindset. It is important to give more to get more. Do not become too possessive as that could be detrimental to your progress; learn to let go.

OCTOBER

You will be energized and eager to take on new beginnings. I see you all geared up and charged to put your ideas into action. Do that, as these ideas or thoughts will render positive outcomes if acted upon timely. There is a lot of hope and good coming out of these new but small initiatives. If you believe in and nurture these ideas, success is certain.

NOVEMBER

This month will pose certain challenges, especially in case of your work. You may be overwhelmed with work pressure. Take up only as much as you can handle. There is some bit of stress that will ease off towards the end of this month. You may come upon a counsellor, friend or someone senior who will guide you through your problems. This help may come in the form of a person or even a spiritual or religious institution.

DECEMBER

Wealth will make its way to you as you reach the end of the year. This wealth may come through an ancestral property, a lottery or other such sources. You could also be involved in a family marriage or any other auspicious function. If you are expecting news related to work, it's likely to get delayed. There is nothing you can do about this but wait for the right time to come.

LOVE PREDICTIONS

Your love predictions are divided into two parts: the first denotes the love life of an Aries who is already in a relationship and the next predicts the future of a single Aries seeking love.

JANUARY

The news in matters of the heart is not so good as you step into the year. There is a revelation that will come forth and it may shatter the dream castle you have so strongly built. This is the result of a long-drawn haul which will reveal itself this *January*. It's time you seriously worked on your love issues before they blow out of proportion.

The single Aries will undertake extensive travel and will chance upon someone interesting. There is good news coming your way if you are single and willing to explore.

FEBRUARY

You will have to strike a balance in your life in general to ensure everything is smooth sailing in matters of the heart. You will be seen juggling two important aspects of your life: one is your lover and the other is something just as important. Respite will come in time but multitasking is inevitable. Do not take your love life for granted.

The single Aries will be exploring life overseas, where international travel will help you connect with someone exciting. You are ready to embark on a journey in love, and I see that something is going to culminate soon.

MARCH

Make it a point to talk to your partner and communicate whatever is on your mind. Listening skills can also go a long way in resolving issues. This month, simply focus on listening to your partner and speak up when needed.

If you are seeking a lover, then this month may mean a time to take a break and focus on yourself internally. You may not be feeling up for anything in this area and some time off will help in coming back feeling rejuvenated.

APRIL

You may choose to put an end to something that isn't right in your relationship. You must do as your heart guides you to. Take a stand; I see that it is much-needed. You may have to be assertive and clear in your decision to stop what you think isn't working out.

If you are looking for love, then this month your wish shall come true. I see you achieving conquest over your love life and you shall get the one you desire.

MAY

There is victory and happiness in your love life this month. Your stand was right and you will feel victorious about the way the situation panned out. Your partner and you will feel loved, and there will be a renewed sense of respect and belonging.

The single Aries may witness a heartbreak or other such disappointment. Something or someone may let you down and you will come to realize that it was never to happen. This news or revelation may be a little hurtful.

JUNE

Your relationship will witness some difficult times. An arrangement is about to come to an end. This decision will be difficult but inevitable. You will both choose to end what may not be working for you.

The single Aries will meet someone interesting in a marriage or an engagement function. Your presence in such an event will offer a breakthrough opportunity to find someone who may just be Mr or Miss right.

JULY

Don't expect your beloved to read your mind. If there is something you wish to communicate, do so at the earliest. Your partner is not a mind reader. On the whole, your relationship will move into a more stable and comfortable zone.

If you are seeking love, you must get over your past. The past is history, don't go back in time and lose the beautiful present. Get in the moment and take control of your life. You shall find someone better than whom you had once.

AUGUST

Your love life will witness new beginnings and happy moments this month. There is a lot to look forward to in general, which will boost your love life and help you overcome any differences with your partner. I see you ready and in control with your love-related thoughts. This a good space to be in.

The single Aries has a lot to be grateful for. Learn to give before you ask something. You must thank the universe for all that you have and trust it to help you achieve whom you truly deserve.

SEPTEMBER

You have everything you need in your love life – happiness, stability and joy. This is the time to throw parties and indulge in everything that pleases you and your beloved. You will be seen amidst people, making merry and celebrating your love life.

The single Aries should stop being conventional and traditional in approach. You must adapt to what is needed and what is trending. Old beliefs will only prove to be detrimental in your search to find the person you so desire.

OCTOBER

Your love life will be at the brink of a new beginning. You may have initiated a new arrangement such as a marriage, engagement or some other decision that will bring forth newness, which has its own risk and thrills. With help from your partner, you are ready to take on whatever life throws at you.

If you are single, then look out for someone exciting coming along this October, who will sweep you off your feet. This person is honest and will love you for who you are. You should be yourself and it is best to be truthful with him or her from day one.

NOVEMBER

You have nothing to ask for and your wish in love shall come to pass. Go forth and celebrate this blessing; show gratitude to your partner and the universe for this beautiful gift of love.

The single Aries will continue to attract someone emotional and loving this month. This new person is a poet, sensitive and exceptionally emotional. Be soft and gentle in your approach.

DECEMBER

It is important to make a few changes and accept some compromises in order to keep the happiness and balance maintained in your relationship. You will have to bring about certain changes which may initially prove to be a little undesirable; but trust me, they will prove to be rewarding in the long run.

The single Aries will witness a new beginning and, as the year comes to an end, I see you getting ready to do what is most needed – explore love and take the leap of faith!

HEALTH PREDICTIONS

JANUARY

Chances are you are overdoing something and putting undue pressure on your body and mind. It's time you took it slow and went with the flow. Overworking will only add to your issues. It is best to relax and take it easy. Times are about to change and whatever occurred so far will change in due course. This change is positive and you can expect good returns when it comes to your health.

FEBRUARY

You will be overwhelmed with life and all the pressure that comes along. Once again, February is a month to slow down and avoid overworking. Be careful with the pressure that comes with work. The good news is that towards the end of the month, you will receive rewards for all your hard work related to health. You will achieve the result you set out.

MARCH

This month will bring in cheer and good news. You will be happy with the way your health looks this month, and there are more than enough reasons to celebrate your good fitness level. Avoid binging and stay close to your health goals. You will chance upon something form the past: a walk down memory lane or an old acquaintance. This chance meeting will connect the dots when it comes to your health.

APRIL

You must watch your health this April. Situations may get worse from where you already are, in case of chronic ailments. The tendency to feel defeated, anxious, sad and left-out may prevail. You must stay strong and overcome these mental blocks. Your test results or the outcome that you have been awaiting is likely to get delayed. You will get the news when time is right.

MAY

You will initiate a new course, routine, treatment or exercise to better your health. This will be one which you probably haven't taken up before. The decision to initiate something new like this will have its own thrills and risks, but the journey ahead is exciting and you must go with the flow. As the month ends, your health will only get better. I see you involved in some happy functions and events this month, which will boost your health.

JUNE

You are stressed about certain things and this begins to take a toll on your health. There is a lot of emotional stress due to issues in personal life or other aspects of life in general. You will have to take precautionary measures. You may encounter mental issues like depression, anxiety and apprehension. A woman's intervention is seen. She shall come to your aid and help you overcome these mental and emotional blocks.

JULY

There is news coming your way this month. It is likely to be good and shall boost you mentally to keep moving forward. Progress and good health will be evident. I see you indulging in a little bit extra. This is good after all you have been through but don't throw away your success by an uncalled-for binge. Watch your indulgence and keep it within your limits.

AUGUST

A big change is set to sweep you off your feet. A transformation of some kind is on the way. You will be seen ending something, only to initiate a renewal. Let's term this your second chance or an inevitability. You will start a new initiative in health this August owing to the change that has come along. It's advised you stay strong, mentally and spiritually, to get by these changes.

SEPTEMBER

You are juggling two important elements of your health. This may mean either your work and personal life or any two opposing elements. This juggling isn't going to be easy and may take a toll on you physically but continue to multitask as I see respite coming along in a bit. You also need to pay some attention to balancing your life. If this imbalance is corrected, it can bring a lot of peace. Watch your work timings and figure out a way to spend some time with loved ones and to do the things you love.

OCTOBER

Some sudden issues will crop up in your health this month. You may have to put your best foot forward and hang in there. You need to separate your work and personal life. Do not bring the stress back home. More importantly, your emotional issues could be causing a lot of your current health problems. You must look into your past and the present to see if you have been holding onto any negative emotions of guilt, anger, failure or hurt. Let them go if you truly want to feel better.

NOVEMBER

Some news that you have been waiting for shall come. The month ends well; you will be seen spending quality time with your loved ones and thanking the universe for such wonderful blessings.

DECEMBER

As the year comes to an end, you will be ready to start with a new-found enthusiasm. You are ready to bring about some changes in your personal life, especially your love life, and are serious about chalking out positive health goals. You can easily achieve what you have set out to do but know that there is some hardwork required. But saying so, you have all it takes to win against all odds.

CAREER PREDICTIONS

JANUARY

As the year begins, you are ready to face the challenges and thrills that lie ahead. There is enthusiasm and commitment in your approach towards your career. You are all set to start something new and approach the career resolutions you have set for the year. You are happy and ready to take on what lies ahead. But if you are looking for a job or an assignment, know that the competition is stiff.

FEBRUARY

There is a strong influence of a senior person – an authoritative man – in your work this month. He is determined, driven and a task master. You will have to up your game and do as guided by him. There is an element of boredom that creeps into your work this month. You are beginning to blame others. My advice is: you should first question your own efforts and intention before blaming others.

MARCH

Listen to your inner voice, it is trying to guide you. You must pay close attention to your intuition. If situations are risky, simply follow your gut. It will guide you to the safest decision. A woman will play an important role in your career this month. She is strong-willed and stubborn. You must know when to put a limit to her influence.

APRIL

Some disturbing revelations will surface this month. Situations don't look that good. If you are unhappy with your job or the people around, you must consider acting upon the difficulties and moving on. If not, then be ready for tough decisions coming ahead. You are about to witness a big change that will set the course for progress thereafter. But something must end for a new beginning. This change isn't easy and you must have an appetite to digest it.

MAY

You seem to be constrained and limited in your thoughts and ideas. Something is holding you back from achieving your full potential. Look closely – you may be limiting yourself with your own beliefs. You must break free if you desire success. There is news coming along, which will open up an avenue for better ideas and a medium to channel your creativity.

JUNE

I see the same limiting beliefs holding you back from success. You must break free and watch your mind's antics. Most of the negativity you face this month is your mind's game. Stay alert and be on your guard. A woman will influence your work positively. She is here to help you and will collaborate to achieve greater objectives.

JULY

You are buzzing with positive ideas and thoughts related to your career. You must act upon them and put them into action. Give them life and you shall be astonished with their potential. However, you seem to be going in the opposite direction towards the end of the month. You are feeling left out and dejected with the way situations have panned out. Your increment or appraisal may have not gone that well and this will leave you feeling disappointed.

AUGUST

There is progress this August and your work picks up. You undertake a lot of land travel to increase business or profits. You are in for some positive developments as the wheel of fortune begins to turn in your favour. Times are about to change and everything that wasn't right before will be corrected and reversed. Happy times are here again.

SEPTEMBER

Do not lose heart or interest in your work. You are questioning yourself and others in your workplace. It's best to look within to correct our own thinking patterns and attitudes. This is the best way to approach work this month. Look at the glass as half-full, not half-empty. A change in perspective is needed. There is some risk involved in your work by the end of the month. Watch where you are headed and do not trust people easily, especially a woman. Play your cards right and follow your intuition.

OCTOBER

A woman seems to be strongly influencing your career once again. This influence cannot be called positive. Use diplomacy, you should know how to tackle her. There is news coming along which I believe isn't positive. You must get ready for some sudden bumps that are not going to go down well with you.

NOVEMBER

If you detest your job and are only in it for the job security it promises, then it's high time you took a decision instead of ranting and complaining about the situation. You need to choose to either stay on or quit. Whatever your decision may be, know it is yours and don't crib about it. I see that you will achieve clarity towards the end of this month; you know what needs to be done and how.

DECEMBER

You are in for some good news as we close the year. You will receive a raise, bonus or appraisal that looks very good. Rewards and recognition are a definite this month. You will end the year well. I see you juggling two important elements of your career like two jobs, two bosses or two assignments.

WEALTH PREDICTIONS

JANUARY

While the year kicks in with zest and joy, your finances seem to be going in the opposite direction. You will face a bit of a logjam where money would be stuck or slow. Many of your payments may get delayed or be likely to do so. But this stagnation is only temporary as the month ends on a good note. You will accomplish a goal that will set the wheel of wealth rolling.

FEBRUARY

You must look closely at the way you conduct your finances. There is an imbalance in your income and expenses. You should try to synchronize them before gap widens too much to be reversed. There is a need to change your approach towards wealth. Give more to get more, and give with an open heart in order to increase the flow of money.

MARCH

A woman will help you stabilize your finances. Listen to her and follow her advice. She is strong yet gentle, and will help you accomplish your financial goals within your limits. You may consider an international holiday or similar expenses.

APRIL

You are questioning your finances and seem to be unhappy with the way life has turned out, but you must know that where you are is your own doing. So look at the brighter side of life and figure out ways to improve your finances instead of blaming others for it.

Avoid risky investments this month. It is not the right time to take uncalculated moves. Stay cautious and play it safe.

MAY

Your wealth will improve gradually this month. You will make small but distinct progress which will add to your income. There is an exciting idea or thought in your mind, and you are convinced of its viability: act upon this idea.

JUNE

You will meet an interesting person or financial institution that will guide you better in your finances. This person or institution is here to help you achieve your financial goals. You need to organize your life and balance it well. You must adopt a more traditional approach if you want to walk away with a good pay packet or retirement fund.

JULY

If you are expecting some positive news related to wealth, it is likely to be delayed. You have no control over it and should wait patiently for the time to change. There is a financial arrangement which will come to an end this month. This arrangement was failing to yield returns and therefore its closure is imperative. This decision would be a tough one but must be made considering the odds.

AUGUST

You will come upon someone from your past who will play an important role in shaping your finances in future. This chance meeting will connect the dots for you and lead you to where you wanted to be financially. You must also adopt caution if there is even a fraction of doubt in your mind about any investment plan or such avenues. It's best to investigate the medium thoroughly before taking it up.

SEPTEMBER

This month is a rather positive one where I see you happy and accomplished. You will be spending some quality time with your loved ones and financial matters will go as planned. But wealth is all about mindset, do not pay heed to the negative thoughts that creep into your mind towards the end of the month. Only you can bring about a change if needed.

OCTOBER

You have to watch your back and know the areas where you are putting your money. Do not trust people easily and be forewarned about situations taking a dramatic turn. Invest cautiously and scrutinize every detail. There must be no room left for speculation. The month ends well and you will overcome the bad time.

NOVEMBER

If you desire a certain financial gain, then it isn't going to be easy achieving it. There are a lot of takers and you will have to fight out the competition. However, I see the month ending with a defeat. Something in your financial matters may not have gone the way you thought it would, but there is nothing you can do except going with the flow.

DECEMBER

You may decide to renovate or refurbish your house as long as your debt is in control. Take up only as much as you can repay. Your finances look good as we approach the end of the year. You shall accomplish your heart's desire and achieve the one thing you truly believed could change the face of your finances. You are in for some happy times!

Taurus – Hierophant
20 April–20 May

Ʉ

Taurus is practical and logical. You are sturdy, stable and dependable, just like your element earth. Loyalty and honesty supersede your other qualities, making you the perfect friend, one who can give unbiased opinions and guidance. Everyone needs a counsellor or a shrink sometimes, and mine is the Hierophant!

Taurus is second in line after Aries. In tarot, Hierophant follows the Emperor. After one's quest for power and victory comes a new perspective – the spiritual aspect of life – and the Hierophant does just that; its primary task is to bring in the spiritual perspective, to heal the inside of a person, to help in exploring the real meaning of the being within.

Hierophant is a Greek word: 'Hieros' means sacred and 'phainein' means to reveal. In simpler terms, it means to reveal the secret of the universe, that there is more to life than just materialism. It's the spiritual journey which the Hierophant asserts. If this sounds obtuse, dear Taurus, let's keep it simple. Hierophant means the Pope or a priest who is out there to teach you the basics of humanity, assert religious rituals or lay down principles which have to be followed – the so-called dogmatic approach. His job is to help and guide you towards your lost spiritual self.

Taurus is known for its dependability, perseverance, patience, stability and stubbornness. These qualities are similar to those of a Hierophant. He too is perseverant, patient, stable, dependable and stubborn. He is an earthly sign like the Taurus, gentle and kind; that is why you fit in the role of a Hierophant perfectly. You are in most times of your life an agony aunt or uncle to someone or the other. You are always there as the unofficial shrink, counselling and guiding your friends and others around you. This is the exact role a Hierophant plays, albeit unknowingly. Unconsciously you are the perfect Pope, a counsellor, an advisor. The Hierophant tarot card has a priestly person dressed in a red robe seated on his throne. In tarot, the Hierophant is denoted by the masculine gender. The robe signifies power and authority, and the crown, his kingship and domain. He holds a sceptre in his right hand, which symbolizes his dominion over the mind, body and spirit. Two fingers of his other hand point upward and two downward. This gesture signifies his power and knowledge to manifest change and bring harmony. The key at the bottom of his feet signifies his possession of the key to unlock the gates of knowledge and wisdom. The two figures kneeling at his feet are seen to be keenly grasping his instructions and accepting them unquestioningly. This confirms his assertion, aggression and control over his community. The card bears V – the fifth month of the year – the month of Taurus. In numerology, five is the number of kindness, courage, enthusiasm and sensitivity. This bears a remarkable similarity to you. You too are kind, sensitive, gentle and enthusiastic.

If I were to describe how a Hierophant would be as a normal person in his daily chores or in the roles of a parent, lover or a boss, it would be something like this: Hierophant is a very good parent. The qualities of being a patient teacher, guide and counsellor come quite naturally to you. You set a very good example by following the rules set by your community and, in most cases, advocate their rituals and beliefs. You are a good parent and mentor. As a lover, you are gentle and kind, understanding and dependable and, most importantly, a faithful companion. Your honesty takes you a long way and makes you a stable and dependable partner. As a boss, you are very encouraging. You are a perfect shrink, someone whom your colleagues, subordinates or seniors can relate to even on a personal level. You make people comfortable and they open up to you like a book. You are frank and helpful, which makes you approachable and likeable to your team.

But there can also be a flip side to this. The orthodox and dogmatic nature of the Hierophant can influence the gentle Taurus very negatively. As a negative parent, you can be overly disciplined, have an orthodox and conventional outlook, and an unwillingness to change and adapt to your family's changing needs. As a lover, the negatives can spring up as stubbornness in dealing with your spouse and wanting to have your way. As a boss, you can be, at your negative best, a dogmatic ruler offering very little or no flexibility to your team players, and instilling wrongful and dishonest values in them. Don't be shocked by this fact. Everyone has a dark side and so do you. You need to balance yourself. The good news is that you may exhibit this dark side in your physical and mental characteristics but never in your spirit. When it comes to the spiritual, you are a winner. Spiritualism comes way too easy to you because of your nature. You are cut out to be a knowledgeable counsellor, a teacher or a *gyaani*. If you don this role in one or more aspects of life, you will definitely realize yourself.

As Taurus, the Hierophant, you have a lot waiting for you in 2019. This book will take you through the future through five different aspects: Monthly predictions, Love, Health, Wealth and Career.

MONTHLY PREDICTIONS

JANUARY

The year starts off very well for the spiritualist Hierophant. You will be in for some good times as you step into *January*. You may receive an unexpected sum of money, and your business or work will be going quite well. Money will definitely not be a problem right now. You may also consider moving houses or buying one this month. Marriage and other happy events are on the cards.

FEBRUARY

You are about to change the course of your actions for something bigger and better. The transition may be a little difficult but the outcome will be great. Go along with the change that will come with a wave of actions that will require to be carried out immediately. Put your thoughts and ideas into life to make the most of this opportunity.

MARCH

An authoritative man will play an important role in your life this month. He is headstrong and difficult to be convinced. It is best to adapt a gentle approach in dealing with this person. The last few days of March will be difficult. You spend sleepless nights worried about certain things that probably don't even exist. These thoughts are fictitious and you must let them go.

APRIL

You are very creative and sentimental this month. You feel loved and the urge to give back love will be strong. This is a happy month for you where you are mentally stable and secure, at least from where you were in the last month. Overseas travel, prosperity and happiness awaits you in April. A news of childbirth too may come along.

MAY

You are at your happiest when you step into May. Your wish shall come to pass if you truly believe in it. So close your eyes, wish for something desirable and see how the universe conspires to make it a reality. Your work looks good too. There is news of a job offer or something positive coming your way.

JUNE

New beginnings and initiative in your work will lead to more wealth, and bring about greater financial stability. You are geared up to make this happen and keen to act upon your ideas. However, you might have to juggle two jobs, two sources of finances or two aspects of your life to do so. Multitasking is the key to success at this moment.

JULY

You will come upon a spiritual experience, a person or an institution that will lead you into something very experiential. This person may be a counsellor or even a friend who brings about a much-needed change in perspective. There is an element of charity in your cards this month. You must give more to get more.

AUGUST

Do not hold on to the ghosts of the past. You must learn to let go; what occurred in the past is history. You may choose to end an arrangement as it may not have worked in your favour. This was the only solution considering the odds. It's best to end an arrangement which has rendered no return to either you or the other party involved. This decision is tough but needed.

SEPTEMBER

Money, health, prosperity and good news is on its way. After the end comes a new beginning. You are in for some pleasant news this September. Marriage and motherhood could also grace you if that has been your wish. Your work will look good and victory is certain after a long battle. You deserve every bit of success.

OCTOBER

You will don the creative cap and churn something remarkable. Use your creative streak to create something exciting and incredible. You are feeling loved and let that love flow through your work. You will undertake overseas travel for either leisure or work. There is an element of happiness and joy all through this October.

NOVEMBER

Money makes its way to you. Your business and work will all be going well. Use the surplus in a good way. Let your money make more money for you. You may consider starting a business this month if that has been on your mind. Your past shall play an important role in your life this month. Something or someone will connect the dots and lead you to the goal.

DECEMBER

You shall recover from all the deficits you have faced so far. Life is good as you come to the end of the year. You must remember you have a strong mind which, if it wills, can accomplish the greatest tasks. Use this inner strength to bring to life your deepest and greatest dreams. A decision would have to be made this month which may lead to a predicament. Think it through before you make the final call.

LOVE PREDICTIONS

Your love predictions are divided into two parts. The first paragraph addresses the already committed Taurus whereas the latter talks about the ones who are single.

JANUARY

The already committed and in love Taurus will face some difficulties this month. Conflicts and interpersonal issues will be on the rise between you and your partner. The fact of the matter is that your partner will have his or her way. You may feel defeated and let down by your partner but this phase is only temporary.

The single Taurus should get ready for a big change that will set the course for the future. The new beginning that life presents now shall help you find the One soon.

FEBRUARY

Your relationship looks positive this month. There is love, respect and equality between the two of you. You both seem to be happy and totally in sync with each other. February is a rather happy month filled with love for the lucky Taurus.

If you are seeking love, then a knight in a shining armour is about to sweep you off your feet. Get ready to meet the Mr Perfect or Ms Right.

MARCH

You may have started something new in your life and this shall influence your love life positively. You are back in the game of love and small baby steps will make a huge difference. Consistent work and focus can yield rewards, and this is exactly what you must do in your love life.

The single Taurus seems to be living in the past. You must let go of your baggage to make a fresh start. You are here and that is what should be your focus. Only by being in the present can you attract the right partner.

APRIL

This month is all about new beginnings and initiatives. Your love life too will be the product of enthusiasm and efforts. There is an eagerness and willingness to work on it to scale it up. This is the right attitude to have as long as you put these ideas into motion.

The single Taurus will see the end of something that may have led to something remarkable in his or her love life. Nevertheless, this end was important as it would lead to the new beginnings.

MAY

This is a great month for the Taurus who is already in a relationship. You and your partner will be completely in love and harmony. There is affection, selfless love and respect for each other. In fact, your love life will only progress from here.

The single Taurus must be patient. If you are awaiting potential prospects, it shall take some more time for this to come to pass. There is a delay in what you may have thought would work out.

JUNE

Your work will play an important role in your love life this month. Do not get so carried away with work that you ignore your beloved. Regular communication and breaks will only instil joy and faith in your relationship.

There is a need for balance in your life if you are seeking love. A lopsided life will affect the prospects of your love life. Therefore, correct the imbalance to get to where you want to be in love.

JULY

If you feel you are stuck in an unhappy relationship or situation in your love life, it's time you took control and acted upon what you think is right. Take corrective measures instead of whining. Also, stay away from negative influences that could influence your love life negatively. One of you in the relationship could be trying to control the other. This is not a good place to be in. Don't dominate or get dominated.

The single Taurus may witness the end of something that could have led to new possibilities in love, but this end was imperative. You must simply accept it and start from scratch.

AUGUST

You may choose to put an end to something that is not all right in your relationship. Certain things need to be put in place and you may decide to do just that in your relationship. It's best to do this gently.

The single Taurus may feel defeated as things may not go as planned or imagined. Your expectations may disappoint you, and this is going to be a challenging phase.

SEPTEMBER

There is an imbalance in your relationship which needs immediate correction. You are torn between two opposing elements like work and love or two options in love. Don't try to brush this situation under the carpet as it will eventually erupt into something big. It is advised you choose the more important option and correct the imbalance.

The single Taurus will witness some happy moments this month. You will initiate a new love affair which could turn into something more serious if the parties involved exert the right will.

OCTOBER

You will face some kind of disappointment or difficulty this month. Not everything shall be smooth sailing. You are going to feel dejected, let down and hurt. Your actions or your partner's may be too hurtful for the other. Stay strong.

If you are looking for love, then this month is going to be a challenging one. You are going to feel lonely and left-out. Do not submit to the negative thoughts your mind throws at you, it's only a phase and shall pass.

NOVEMBER

November will be a month of difficulties. A certain truth shall surface and will leave you shattered. Your relationship is going to face a turbulent time. Not everything is as true as it may seem on the outside. You will have to pick up the pieces and start all over again.

The single Taurus must avoid jumping to quick conclusions and passing incorrect judgements. This is the month to watch your thoughts and wait for the right opportunity, which will come in due course.

DECEMBER

Conflicts and interpersonal issues will pose a serious threat to your relationship. If you are unhappy about something then it is advised to speak up and clear the air. This counterargument will cause some tension and make the situation bitter. You must do so honestly and assertively.

The year ends well for the single Taurus. I see an authoritative and endearing woman stepping into your life. You will be smitten by her and, if worked upon correctly, this may lead to something more concrete and lasting. The single woman Taurus too shall get an opportunity to explore love originating from her workplace.

HEALTH PREDICTIONS

JANUARY

The year starts off with a reminder: the universe wants you to count your blessings. Your health may not be all that you want it to be but it's still better than most people. You need to look at the brighter side of life and take it easy. A break will come in handy from time-to-time. There is an emotional zest in you – a willingness to do something new and achieve your health goals. This approach is great provided you work on it.

FEBRUARY

Emotions will play an important role in your health this month. You are bound to feel rather vulnerable and sensitive towards yourself and others. It is all right to share your feelings and give love to those who deserve it. A man will play an important role in your care. His knowledge and affection will stabilize your health problems. There is a reason to cheer as we end this month. I see you involved in parties, functions, etc., which will keep you motivated and happy.

MARCH

You must be patient with yourself. Do not get impatient if you don't see results. It is our side of the bargain to put in our best, and the universe will give rewards when the time is right. Be easy on yourself and work towards your goals patiently. The month ends well and I see you accomplishing an impossible health goal. This will bring about much-needed peace and calm. You deserve every bit of this accomplishment.

APRIL

Your work place is going act as the devil. It is best to take it easy, and to try not to get overwhelmed with the pressure and stress. Take up only as much as you can handle. There is a note of caution in April. Do not trust people easily when it comes to medical advice and intervention. Take a second opinion, if needed. There is a possibility of deceit and treachery.

MAY

The key to stability in health is balance. You must balance your lifestyle and take a close look at the way you conduct your well-being. If you have the tendency to hold on to the past, then let go. Anger, resentment, guilt and remorse will only make you sick and ail you further. Try to live in the moment and the clutches of past will loosen their grip on you.

JUNE

You will begin a partnership with another person who will help you achieve better fitness levels. This is mostly a short-term association and will yield good results. However, most of your health issues have an underlying emotional and spiritual cause. You must look into your life and choose to let go of pent-up emotions or issues that are holding you back from living in the moment.

JULY

The way you started something new last month, this month I see you ending one such association. The arrangement didn't go down well and might have failed to reap the benefits you thought it would. Ending this arrangement isn't going to be easy but it is something you must do. This will cause some emotional issues and you will get overwhelmed with the way situations unfold. Stress from work and other areas will also bring you down.

AUGUST

You will decide to take charge of your life, especially your mental health. You will choose happiness over other emotions and, I must say, it is indeed a good start. You look charged, rejuvenated and ready to take on what problems life poses. Your work and professional life affect your health greatly. This month you have something new to look forward to at work.

SEPTEMBER

You will meet a counsellor, a traditional healer or a therapist who will come to your aid. This month could also connect you with a spiritual institution that may bring about a change in perspective. This is crucial, considering your spiritual side. Your suffering is soon about to come to an end. I see a stark recovery where the will to fight back overrides everything else. This is a mindset which you will adopt and thereby experience complete and total recovery.

OCTOBER

A very important decision needs your attention. But this decision is difficult as you have to make a choice from many options. You are confused, flustered and in a fix. This state is likely to cause some stress but what lies ahead will bring some respite. I see that you will start a new health regime, routine or treatment that you haven't done before. There are risks involved but none that you cannot deal with.

NOVEMBER

You need to watch your health. Certain revelations will surface either in health or life that will emotionally devastate you. You have to have a strong heart to deal with what lies ahead. Take care of your health and ensure nothing goes unnoticed. Get to the bottom of any issue which you believe may turn its ugly head onto you. Life will defeat you and such will be your state. You will feel beaten and haggard, and it will be a challenging phase. But what you must look forward to is the fact that nothing is permanent, and your situation too shall change.

DECEMBER

You are going to face some health challenges this December but stand a good chance to beat this issue. You are strong willed and determined, which will help you overcome most health issues. The year ends with you taking complete charge and control of your life. You will meet a woman who will play an important role in shaping your health.

CAREER PREDICTIONS

JANUARY

The year starts off with feelings of rejection and disappointment. You might have faced a defeat or felt discredited or disregarded by your seniors at your workplace. Another way to look at the present situation is to stop possessing negative ideas, and thoughts about yourself and your work. Don't turn into your own enemy or inflict torture on yourself. The job or assignment you seek will have tough competition. You stand a good chance provided you play fair.

FEBRUARY

You will take control of your professional life and get back in action. I see you strategizing and devising new plans to achieve your career goals. This is great considering a woman is coming to your aid and helping you out there. There is some mental upheaval in store for you, which you might have to factor in this month. Keep sadness at bay, and use all your creative juices to guide you out of emotional entrapment. This is also the time where you will be at the peak of your creative best.

MARCH

When everything fails, hope comes to your aid. Stay positive and hold on to your belief in good things. It is only a matter of time before situations will begin to change. You need to believe in your potential. In fact, by mid-March you will begin to see some positive developments. Recovery is definite and it is all due to your will to succeed.

APRIL

A decision has to be made but the choice is too hazy. You seem to be confused and stressed about what to do next. This decision would either make or break your career. Hence, sufficient time must be given to the decision-making process. The good news is that I see you initiating a new venture by the end of this month. This only goes to say you have made a choice to start off in spite of the risks and uncertainties involved in the new project.

MAY

If you have the tendency to question yourself at every juncture, then you are becoming an impediment in your progress. Defeat and failure is part of the game, and how one copes will depend on his or her potential to stay calm and strong. Don't jump to quick conclusions and use the help of a woman who will come along your way. The month will end well with work picking up gradually and you will be completely incharge of it.

JUNE

I have noticed a pattern in your career predictions where your negative mindset is playing with your peace of mind. You must let go of pessimistic thoughts and focus on ideation. Do not succumb to mind games. You may begin to spend sleepless nights worried about issues that don't really exist and are all in your head. Despite all odds, the month ends well and I see rewards coming in in the form of money and recognition.

JULY

A man will play an important role in your career this July. He could be your senior or boss who is willing to extend help and guide you under the present circumstances. Do not leave room for mistakes and get serious about your work. Times are going to be challenging as I see situations turning into a dark mess. You may feel threatened and isolated amongst people at your workplace. Don't trust people easily and it would be wise to say – watch your back.

AUGUST

You will be tensed and confused about your career as we step into this month, and may feel distorted with all that is happening around you. There is a lot of emotional stress hovering in the background. You may feel attacked by co-workers or people in general. It's best to stay calm and handle the situation patiently. Follow your instincts. The month ends well and you will see the silver lining. Stay hopeful and stay positive.

SEPTEMBER

This month is very good for your career as I see you accomplishing all of your career goals. Your targets will be achieved and you will complete the work you had chosen to do. This is great as it will set the course for new developments. A woman will play an important role in your career. She is headstrong and dominating. It is always good to draw a limit to people's unwanted intervention. Know where to say no.

OCTOBER

If you are unhappy with your current job, then it's time you took charge and acted upon it. If it's a thankless or boring job, then you should work on fixing this. It's never too late and now may just be the time to bring about the amends which were long due. The arrangement that you are in may conclude this month. You will choose to end it so that you can follow your passion. This would be a difficult but good decision.

NOVEMBER

You will get good news of a job offer, assignment or contract. This will lead to new ways of generating wealth and will therefore light you up. You have a lot to look forward to in November, as this month is the genesis of beautiful opportunity.

DECEMBER

You will initiate a new venture or some other new beginning. This venture or start-up will need all of your strength, intellect, commitment and discipline. You need to believe in your dream and go all out in making it a reality. The year ends with a message where tarot wants you to learn to let go, especially in money matters. Remember: the more you give or share, the more you will get. So give with an open heart and you will see the wheel of fortune turn in your favour.

WEALTH PREDICTIONS

JANUARY

As you start the year, you may face some difficult times with your finances. Your cash flow is going to be tight. It is advised to plan ahead for the rainy day. Your work could be responsible for the low cash flow. The month ends well and I see you attracting something very important and desirable. This may mean a better job, better pay, bonus, investment returns, etc.

FEBRUARY

There is an imbalance in your income and expenses that you must correct. This imbalance can be corrected if you plan your finances well. Don't indulge in expensive affairs and manage your cash flow effectively. Try to put money away only in places where it is most needed. You will have too many expenses and too little income in hand to manage them all. Therefore, prioritize your spends and use money prudently. This phase is once again going to be a bit tough but if you use your resources well, it can be manageable.

MARCH

Good times are here again. Your finances will pick up and most of your immediate monetary worries will settle. You will begin to see a positive change in your sources that bring in wealth. A change is about to come which will be responsible for setting the course for better and improved finances. But this change comes with a wave of unsettling feelings but things will eventually fall in place.

APRIL

A man will play an important role in shaping your finances. His influence is good as long as you know how and when to limit it. Listen to him but apply your analysis to his ideas. The month will end with good news. You may receive a good return on investment and similar possibilities will fall in place.

MAY

The wheel of fortune is turning in your favour. All that was not well will change and situations will begin to move to your benefit. Luck will suddenly smile upon you and your finances will be on an upswing. This will bring forth recovery from any deficits that you have faced so far. Life in general would be good with money favouring you in May.

JUNE

The news is good as I see wealth coming in this month. If you are involved in a business or any other arrangement, it will be very good this month. You may receive a raise, an unexpected bonus or increments. You may also consider starting something of your own with the surplus money you have earned. This will uplift your spirits and help you attract more wealth.

JULY

July is yet another happy month for you where you may undertake overseas travel and plan holidays. There is money to do this and prosperity in general will be gracing you. However, do look out for that negative mindset that leaves you feeling withdrawn and questioning your financial position. At the end of the day, your status is what you make of it. Therefore, it's best to think positive and be grateful for what you have rather than blaming destiny and circumstances.

AUGUST

You are stuck between two opposing elements, which is creating an imbalance in your finances. You are actively involved in two financial avenues, and it is sucking the life out of you. You must choose one and let go of the other. Funding both may not be a good idea. The good news is that whatever may be the case now, the final outcome is positive.

SEPTEMBER

This is a fantastic month as your wish is about to come true. Your wealth is on an upswing. You will have all that money can buy, along with a stable and happy emotional state. There is stability, success and financial rewards packed into this September.

OCTOBER

History repeats itself as I see the wheel of fortune once again turning in your favour. Wealth will come in unexpected ways and this will change the phase of your destiny. This is lady luck shining on you and you must make the most of the opportunities and abundance that comes through. There is stark recovery from any or all financial deficits that you might have been facing lately. This happiness and success is the outcome of a strong will and determination which only a Taurus exhibits. Keep up the good work!

NOVEMBER

You will be involved in happy events, and may receive money from long-forgotten ancestral properties or sources of wealth where luck plays a major role. Fortune continues to bestow its best on you as I see you happy and joyous. There is a certain emotional stability and a wealth mindset that you have established, and it will help attract more opportunities.

DECEMBER

Don't let your mind get the better of you. You have come too far to throw all the good away by harnessing negative thoughts. Stay positive and believe in your dream, whatever the odds may be. Time is testing you and, more importantly, your mind is up to its antics. The year ends well with you taking charge of both your thoughts and work. This is good considering the odd beginning you had this month. You will be back in the game.

Gemini – Lovers
21 May–20 June

♊

Gemini is the third sign of the zodiac but the first to use human figures in its representation. In tarot, Gemini is described by the Lovers card. As the name denotes, this card is all about love, choices, temptation, indulgence, lust, greed and pleasure. It is a good mix of all the characteristics of the opposites like the yin and yang, or male and female, and is therefore more popularly known as the dual card. Lovers stands for duality. It is a combination of the characteristics of the twins but in antithesis. That is why the card from the Rider-Waite deck has a man and a woman, the opposites that make up God's creation. This card brings in the qualities of the opposites into perspective when we talk about its association with Gemini. Like the twins in the zodiac's representation of Gemini, Lovers fit in perfectly with the explanation of duality inherent to this sign. Read on to know why you are dual yet one in tarot.

To begin with, let us understand the physical characteristics of the Lovers card. When you look at the card you see an angel with arms outstretched, looking at the opposites created by God – a woman and a man. In tarot, these characters are Adam and Eve. The angel is Raphael, blessing God's finest creation with Love and Air. Raphael is the angel of Air, which is also the element of Gemini. Air stands for communication and Gemini is bestowed with the best communication skills by Raphael. The angel's cloak, purple in colour, denotes royalty and the importance given to communication in today's world. The man and woman standing on a plane of earth, greenish in colour, imply the fertile land of happiness and eternal promises. The cloud from which the angel emerges is the power of the Universal Energy. Behind the woman, the tree bearing five fruits symbolizes the five senses. This woman is a sensual creation as denoted by this tree of senses. It also has a serpent that reminds us of the story of Adam and Eve. The nudity of the two, the proof of this story, later became an act of shame and misery for the human form. Behind the man is a tree of twelve flames. This tree stands for his passion and the twelve flames for the twelve zodiac signs. He looks at her while she looks at the angel; the posture establishes a direct connection among the three forms – the human form (the man), the unconscious (the woman), and the super conscious (the angel). The Lovers card is thus a complete trilogy of Body, Mind and Soul. Due to the male and female characteristics of this card, it is described as the card of duality which is in complete sync with the twin features of Gemini. The card is numbered six for the sixth month of the year, June. Six is more importantly the number of Harmony and as you can see, the elements of man and woman in the Lovers card establish complete harmony. This is the most important trait of a Gemini. Whatever the circumstances, they can establish complete harmony and peace in difficult times.

The angel Raphael has blessed you with communication skills, thereby making you witty, intelligent and sharp. You are very good with words and can please or displease people at will. If you choose an industry where communication is important, you will definitely score above the rest. You are outspoken and easily liked, or rather loved, by others. You love beauty, are attracted to beautiful people and things, and tend to get carried away by it. This probably is your greatest tool and your biggest downfall. You tend to sway from the real to the unreal very easily. This primarily happens due to the contradictory thoughts that race across your mind in any given situation; at one moment you are sane, and highly illogical the very next. Your answer to a given situation may be positive and a moment later, it could turn negative. There will be no logical explanation to this kind of immediate shift in your thought but it does frequently happen in your case. This is the dual nature of your personality and your card, and it tends to put you in a fix, especially in matters of the heart.

You are an intuitive soul. The woman's presence in the Lovers Card emphasizes the power of senses, especially of intuition and knowledge. You use this very well in your existence as a Gemini. As a rational thinker, a worshipper of beauty and lover of art, you are charming and appealing to others. The power of senses bestowed upon you makes you a supreme and witty thinker, and the sensual side of the woman brings forth your sexual charm, making you very attractive to the opposite sex in combination; it is your greatest strength in accomplishing everything you want in all aspects of life. The presence of Adam, the male in the Lovers card, denotes the raw passion for love and sensual pleasures. You are very attractive and tend to get carried away by this raw energy. In such cases, you can use your intuition, the woman's energy and the power of logical thinking present in you. This clearly explains how you behave within the dual nature of antithesis. On one hand you have the tendency to fall and on the other, the sanity to think wisely and rise. Spiritually, your only weakness is your superficial side which gets the better of you, making you see only the artificial aspects of life. You only see what your eyes can and not what your soul should. This makes it difficult to establish a spiritual goal, although the Lovers card bears a strong spiritual essence of the trilogy of Body, Mind and Soul. You are full of contradictions and practical knowledge. You need to put the contradictions to rest and give rise to practical and logical thinking to revive the Spirit in you.

So go forth and create your destiny. I hope you have enjoyed knowing yourself through tarot. As Gemini, the Lovers, you have a lot waiting for you in 2019. This book will take you through the future through five different aspects: Love, Health, Wealth, Career and Monthly predictions. I hope this book serves you as a clear guideline to what lies ahead.

MONTHLY PREDICTIONS

JANUARY

The year will start with a break. It may be for leisure or simply to clear your head. The break will definitely give you much-needed clarity. Your career may be taking a beating. You are being pushed into a corner. You feel defeated and lost, and could be considering an exit from your workplace but tarot advises otherwise. You must stay on as times are about to change.

FEBRUARY

A man who is senior in age and authority will come to your aid. His guidance will ease a lot of tension. However, there is a need to balance your life. You must get more organized and disciplined in your approach towards life in general. You could again take a break towards the end of the month, either to recuperate or simply for a short holiday.

MARCH

Do not jump to conclusions and make wrongful judgements. You must take it easy and watch your performance. There is a possibility that others are judging you or that you are being too judgemental. An adamant and dominating male figure could influence your life this month. Keep him at arm's length as his intervention may be more than asked for.

APRIL

An arrangement is about to fail. You may have worked on it but its end was definite. This will only help you evolve and move on in life. You will now be ready to follow your passion and seek out your calling. There is good news coming your way regarding wealth.

MAY

You will sail through most difficulties this month and settle down. The times have changed and May is a stable, peaceful month for you.

A dilemma may appear towards the end of the month where you will be seeking clarity. Take your time and evaluate all the options before making a decision.

JUNE

You will conquer all odds this month. Success is yours after a long battle. You will get your due. You may also consider the purchase of an automobile. Your work will be going rather smoothly except in few instances where you may have to put your best foot forward and be firm about your ideas and thoughts regarding work. It's good to put forward your ideas clearly when the time is right.

JULY

You will come upon a bright idea or thought which, if acted on, can change the course of your destiny. You must move fast and put these ideas to life; they have potential. A senior, a male member from your work, will support you in achieving these goals and work will pick up once again.

AUGUST

Your romantic relationship or a matter close to your heart is about to receive a closure. You have done your best, but it was time to move on and end what was not working out. The news ahead is good where life will present opportunities that can change the course of events for the better in future. One such news is on its way this August.

SEPTEMBER

You will receive heart-breaking news this month. September is going to be a difficult month initially, but it will all be great as you move towards the end of the month. Initial disappointment, heartache and dejections are natural in matters of the heart but as we reach the end of the month, I see you involved in parties, reunions and other events that will keep you motivated and charged.

OCTOBER

You will receive positive news regarding job opportunities, work assignments or a job offer. You will have to multitask between two aspects of life to make the most of the opportunity that has come this month. You could be juggling between two jobs, two people or two aspects of life.

NOVEMBER

You are going to complete the task or work assigned to you. You will earn accomplishments for the job done well. This month is great as I see you in complete control of your life but it is always advisable to go slow, and avoid pushing yourself and others around too much. This may backfire. You must work to your best capacity while keeping note of others' limitations.

DECEMBER

You will be very stressed due to a high-pressure job or work assignment. You may have taken more than you can handle in terms of work. Watch your health and keep the stress levels minimal. You could be overwhelmed with all that work pressure. A new initiative is about to start and, for all you know, you could be working on this initiative. This is great. provided you work within your limits and act fast.

LOVE PREDICTIONS

Your love predictions are divided into two parts. The first paragraph addresses the Gemini who is committed and the second addresses the single Gemini.

JANUARY

There is some amount of stress in your love life this month. You look overwhelmed with all that life is throwing at you as we step into the year, and this takes a toll on your love life. You must take it easy and prioritize important aspects, love being one. Communication and sharing is of prime importance and it will help you ease tensions with your partner.

The single Gemini will be attracted to someone older and senior in authority. You may be tempted to throw this away due to the age gap, but in my opinion you should give it a fair shot.

FEBRUARY

You are about to start something new in your life and this will positively influence your relationship. You are excited, happy and eager to do what you are thinking and this may as well be related to your relationship. You are about to change your course of actions.

The single Gemini may face some problems in finding love. You are feeling restricted and constrained, which is adversely impacting your potential in finding a lover. You must break free from your self-limiting thoughts and beliefs.

MARCH

You will achieve what you had set out to in your love life this March. This means a feeling of accomplishment and conquest. You may finally make a very important decision or take an important step which completes the cycle of your love life. I see happiness and love in your relationship.

The single Gemini would be seen juggling two options of love. Both have potential but only time will tell which of the two is most suited for you. Otherwise, you may also have to make time for love by juggling two important aspects of your life.

APRIL

You will decide to put an end to something which is not right in your relationship. This may be difficult and could have adverse effects, but you seem to have made up your mind. My only advice is to do this gently and lovingly.

The single Gemini will meet someone kind, generous and loving. This is a great sign and you must convey your interest to this person.

MAY

Your relationship will be going well this month. Your partner would be forthcoming and will express his or her intentions of love to you clearly and strongly. There is good chemistry in your relationship. A positive news could also be expected around this time.

The single Gemini is ready to start a new love life and will be in sync with the universe to help in attracting the right partner.

JUNE

Something seems off about your relationship. The chemistry, thrill and passion is missing, and only you can rekindle this aspect of your relationship. This requires some introspection and a need to point fingers at yourself first instead of the other.

You will meet someone exciting and interesting if you are single. This person is authoritative and quick with his or her decisions, with the tendency to call the shots.

JULY

Your relationship is about to take a turn for the good. There is a feeling of renewal which sparks love and passion once again. You are ready to give first, and this attitude will only help your relationship stabilize in the future.

If you are looking for love, this month brings forwards an opportunity to meet the right person. I see accomplishment in love this May. You shall get what you want.

AUGUST

There is an element of doubt, lie or deceit in your relationship. Either you or your partner is not being honest about something and that fact shall reveal itself. You must manage this situation truthfully and assertively to minimize the damage, and make sure there is no room for error.

You shall meet the perfect lover or partner this month. Love, marriage and a union is on your cards. The single Gemini shall get what he or she always desired in love.

SEPTEMBER

You will have quite a few choices before you and an important decision must be made. This phase is directly proportionate to your love life's stability. You could be weighing your choices, one of which will be your partner.

The single Gemini needs to balance his or her life in order to make some progress in love. You need to understand if you are willing to give the time and commitment needed to make room for love.

OCTOBER

You will end your current relationship as it is proving to be hurtful and traumatizing. This relationship isn't working out, in spite of the efforts both parties involved have put in. This decision, although difficult, would have to be made considering the circumstances. It is good for both you and your lover.

You shall be swept off your feet if you are seeking love. A bright, attractive and sensitive individual is about to enter your life.

NOVEMBER

You have to speak your mind and make yourself heard in your relationship. You must put your viewpoint forward and do so when needed. Communication is the key to success in any relationship, including your romantic relationship. Pay attention to your partner's concerns and voice out yours.

This month, the single Gemini shall again meet a commanding and charismatic person. This person is headstrong for the right reasons and will help you arrive at a decision that needed to be made.

DECEMBER

You are all set to initiate a new journey in love. This journey could be starting a relationship, considering marriage, engagement or other steps which will confirm your commitment. This is new, exciting and has its own thrills. You are now ready to embark on this journey of love and, needless to say, stay positive.

The single Gemini will hear good news that will bring in prospects of love this month.

HEALTH PREDICTIONS

JANUARY

Your health looks good as you start the year and you seem to be in great shape. Your health will be at its peak, and I see you making some important decisions to shape it better. There is a male influence in matters of your health this month. He could be a doctor, therapist, health instructor, etc. who is going to be demanding but helpful in nature. You will take complete control of the necessary changes that need to be made to maintain the required health vitals.

FEBRUARY

Balance is the key to success this month. You will have to ensure that your mind, body and spirit are all working in the same direction to deliver a fit and healthy you. Any imbalance will cause your health to deplete. Give some thought and ask yourself if you are maintaining the balance needed. The month ends with certain facts about your health coming to light that may not sound positive. You will be frayed but it's time to take charge and work on the revelations.

MARCH

Your health is about to change for the good. You will witness some stable and healthy times ahead. A woman will influence your health greatly this month, but know where to draw the line to her intervention. She could be a friend, family, spouse or even a therapist.

APRIL

You shall receive a reward for all the hard work you have put in so far in matters of health. You have been working relentlessly and the results are out. They are positive and the vitals will look good. You are once again at the peak of your health. Some indulgence is allowed and you have completely earned it.

MAY

You will reach a point where an important decision must be made regarding health. There is some amount of confusion this month which may take a toll on your health. Keep anxiety and stress at bay, and watch your mental health. You may receive positive news about your health but avoid the grandiose attitude, and do not overdo anything that can become a cause of worry.

JUNE

You will commence something new and different this June. There is a certain treatment, routine or therapy which you will undertake that will set the course for new beginnings in regards to health. This activity or routine is one which you have never undertaken before. This is also the time when a person, such as a healer, or a life changing situation may appear. This event will help you overcome all your ailments and bring about a new perspective on life.

JULY

Things will begin to look up if you stay positive and hopeful. Whatever may be the case now, you must hold on and the situation will soon change. The month ends exactly the way I thought – with happiness and joy. One of your greatest wishes in health comes true and leaves you feeling elated and ecstatic. You will be doing great in health as July ends.

AUGUST

You will meet a sensitive, emotional and helpful woman who will help you overcome your existing ailments or achieve your health goals. Her influence is positive and you can use her help. This is also the time when you should turn to the feminine side of your personality, and show affection and love to your body and mind. Adopt a loving and caring approach. There is some stress towards the end of the month but you will have to hang in there till the situation turns in your favour.

SEPTEMBER

The news is not all good this month. You may face some difficult times in health or life that will cause sadness, hurt and emotional distress. You will have to stay strong and fight. Do not trust people easily and it is always advisable to take a second opinion. There is a major imbalance in your life that needs immediate correction. You must take into consideration what you are overdoing or not doing at all. If there is a confusion between two elements or choices, choose one and let go of the other.

OCTOBER

The month opens with some bad news. You may come across some disappointing news regarding your health or situations in general, especially your love life. Have a strong heart and everything will heal with time. Towards the end of the month you will be working on doing everything right. Start by asking yourself if you are resting enough, eating right and exercising well. These answers will help you chalk out a plan that can boost your overall well-being.

NOVEMBER

You look fit, rejuvenated and charged up. I see you are ready to embark on a journey where everything looks crystal clear. You are clear what actions have to be taken in order to improve your vitals. There is a strong line of recovery this November. If you were down and out, then all of that is about to change. You have overcome the odds with your strong will to fight and this is great. Keep up the spirit!

DECEMBER

There are chances you are overdoing something. Take it easy; especially if you have started a new health routine, exercise, etc. You don't have to rush it. Just enjoy and the results will fall in place. Silence and some peace can bring about a huge respite. The year ends with your health looking up and good. You will be happy with your achievements and this will keep you motivated to do better next year.

CAREER PREDICTIONS

JANUARY

You must conduct yourself in a more diplomatic and strategic way. Avoid being pushy and don't step into your peers or colleagues' workspace. Conflicts may arise but you can manage people tactfully. If you are being interviewed, present yourself with modesty and keep your ego in check. The month ends well though, and you will receive the rewards for your efforts. An influential man will play an important role in your career this month.

FEBRUARY

There is complete clarity in what you want to do in terms of work and you are ready to move on and make those choices that help you achieve your career goals. Your work will be going well and there is much to look forward to. If you must stay back in the same job, adopt an attitude of gratitude as the job supports you.

MARCH

You find it hard to let go and are becoming difficult to deal with. You must not hold on to things that aren't yours, be it power, position or work. This is all temporary and everything in life is subject to change. Let go and see the larger picture. You are somehow feeling trapped and restricted. Your self-limiting thoughts and beliefs are becoming an impediment to your progress, but you can break free from them if you wish to.

APRIL

You will be stuck in a situation where work seems too burdensome and difficult. You may not be up for it and this place isn't where you really want to be. In such a situation, make your decisions clearly and move on. Do not feel anxious, instead, channelize this energy and make the decisions needed to be made. The month ends with absolute clarity about what you want to do next and this will bring forth ideas and opportunities that best fit your requirement.

MAY

Your work will be demanding this month and there will be questions raised regarding your deliverables. It's best to hold your ground and continue to work without any faults and errors. You don't want to give opportunity to be singled out for the wrong reasons. You will start something of your own towards the end of the month. This may be a new business unit or a new job. This is great and you have all it takes to succeed.

JUNE

You are in for some good news this month. A new of job opportunity or opening will come through. I see you travelling overseas in the pursuit of better job openings. This may be temporary or permanent.

JULY

You will come up with some bright new ideas to make life easy for yourself and others. You may also consider leaving your existing job or develop new ideas and thoughts to change the existing work scenario entirely. You are going to land into conflicts with others in your workplace. Handle people carefully and diplomatically. If you are looking for jobs, present yourself with modesty and manage others and your ego well.

AUGUST

A strong authoritative man will play an important role in your workplace this month. He is quick to pass judgements and will scrutinize everything that you have been doing so far but if you manage to work with him, then you have won him for good. There are some issues that will crop up as we end this month. Certain facts will surface that will make your position shaky in the existing set-up.

SEPTEMBER

Your immediate senior or male boss will come to your aid. He is someone who will bail you out and help you recover from deficits. In fact, he will give you something important that can change the course of the outcomes. He may just give you the right opportunity or break you so needed.

OCTOBER

Beware of a person who is stubborn, dominating and difficult to deal with. If these qualities describe your male boss, then managing him is going to be difficult this month. It's purely his way or no other way.

NOVEMBER

A big change is going to sweep you off your feet. This change shall lead to the end of something for something better to come forth. The change was imperative and much-needed. Your work is likely to face some challenges under the prevailing conditions but all you can do is hang on and continue to do your bit. Success is at hand if you stay and fight on.

DECEMBER

You will initiate a new partnership with another person. This venture is short-lived and will be rewarding. But there are too many choices to choose from further into the month. You will find yourself in utter confusion and the choice will become difficult. Think wisely before you make a decision.

WEALTH PREDICTIONS

JANUARY

Your wealth is going to undergo a sea of change as we start the year. A major source of your income would be terminated, only for a big transformation to come along. This may be by choice or by force but it shall work hugely in your favour. Your cash flow therefore will see some shaky times ahead but you have to hold on to the change you see coming along.

FEBRUARY

You will undertake a short partnership with an individual or institution that will turn out fruitful and boost your finances. There are a couple of financial decisions that need to be made and demand your attention. You have to weigh all the choices and make an informed decision to ensure you don't land into trouble.

MARCH

You will consider shifting homes, home purchases or other real estate investments. This is good as March is a favourable month for your finances. I see gradual positive progress as good news in your wealth prospects comes towards the end of the month.

APRIL

You will be doing exceptionally well this month. Your wealth looks good, and you seem to be happy with all that you have earned and achieved so far. This is the best time to count your blessings and give thanks to the universe. An imbalance will cause some problems towards the end of the month. If you are stuck between two opposites, make a quick decision.

MAY

Your finances may not look that strong right now and you may not be able to keep up with your financial commitments but this isn't permanent. All situations change and so will this tight financial scenario. You need to get over your self-limiting beliefs and negative thought pattern. Adopt a millionaire's mindset to attract wealth.

JUNE

It's important to give more to get more. You must open your palm and share money with an open heart to change the present situation. If you have the money, then don't be too sticky about it. Let go and it will come back to you. There is progress and good news coming that will shape your finances for the better.

JULY

Your income and expenses are not in sync this month. There is a very strong imbalance in the way you are conducting your finances. Ensure you use your money prudently and save more. Avoid unnecessary expenses. You will come upon some bright new ideas, especially in matters of work which is the key source of income.

AUGUST

You will either do charity or receive financial aid from someone who is a giver. If you are giving aid, it is great because that will only get more to you and if you are on the receiving end, then the aid shall sort the financial deficits. There is hope for improvement but you need to stay positive. Tarot advises you to look through the darkness, believe that all will eventually be good and it will soon come to pass.

SEPTEMBER

You will make small but gradual progress in your finances this month. You may also come upon some positive news that will help you shape your money matters well. Your work will especially contribute to this progress and I see good stability there.

OCTOBER

The month doesn't start all that well. There could be some negative news or events which will send your finances to rock bottom but there is definite progress from that point onwards. You may have to make some prudent decisions to either avoid what comes along or have a strong backup to withstand these events. The month ends well with unexpected bonus or wealth coming from either ancestral properties, lottery or such sources where luck plays an important role.

NOVEMBER

You will get a good return on your investments and you may just walk away with bonus, incentive or salary raise. This is great and well-deserved. There is a need to be more balanced and organized in the way you conduct your finances. Get more serious and specific about your financial goals. A senior man will be of help here to guide you.

DECEMBER

You are constantly living under fear and negativity. If you are insecure about your wealth or its sources, then let go of such a negative mindset as it isn't doing you any good. You might be spending sleepless nights worried and stressed about your finances when the problems only exist in your head. The year ends with an advice from tarot. Stay positive and hopeful.

Cancer – Chariot
21 June–22 July

♋

You are fourth in the list of zodiac signs. In the journey of tarot, the card that describes you comes right after the Lovers' Card. This means that after you have realized what you truly desire or love, you have to embark on a journey to achieve it. Thus begins a conquest, a journey or a battle to fight for what you want. This conquest is the description of the Chariot card, the card that describes you. Chariot denotes conquest, victory, glory and success. You are a victorious warrior who has set out on a battle to attain your heart's desires. This begins an interesting story of how you do it and whether you succeed or not. Are you always this fearless, like the warrior in Chariot? I will answer these questions as we unravel interesting facts about the Chariot in relation to you. To begin with, let us understand what the Chariot is all about in tarot.

The Chariot card from the Rider-Waite tarot deck has a warrior sitting under a canopy of stars. This implies celestial influence. He wears an armour with two moons, one below either shoulder, denoting the formative period; the armour represents the warrior's hard-headedness. The square-like structure represents planet Earth, where the warrior has to undertake his conquest. The wings on this square are his inspiration for freedom, and the Hindu symbol underneath it along with the black-and-white sphinxes, symbolizes the union of man and woman, positive and negative, the union of the head and the heart. He holds a spear, which symbolizes his power and ruthless confidence. The crown with the star represents his knowledge and wisdom of the mind, body and spirit. The warrior is in command of his chariot, keeping all its elements together, and drives them in oneness towards the battlefield. This illustrates his

54

strength in putting all of his qualities together to achieve his desire. He is a fighter who is in command and rarely loses.

Like the Chariot card, you are always in control of your life. There will never be an instance where you seem confused and unclear about your goals. You have this remarkable quality of channelizing all of your strengths towards attaining the desired goal. This is why you rarely fail. You are well read and are aware of Universal facts, as seen in the warrior's formative knowledge, and the celestial influence of the moon and stars. You are hard-headed like the warrior's shield and know the difference between good and bad like the Sphinxes of the chariot. You are clever and clear about what you want and how to get there. The chariot implies movement and reflects one of your most important traits. You move swiftly from one goal to another with complete clarity, and will hardly ever stagnate or feel saturated. You will do new things that will set newer and bigger goals for you. You are an emotional soul, sensitive and easily hurt. This is why the warrior shields himself with heavy armour; as does your zodiac sign, the crab, with its shell. You like to show yourself as tough but that's only your outer shell; inside, you are soft and this is why you avoid confrontations, preferring to work alone to attain your goals. You are a one-man army, like the warrior of the Chariot. You don't have an army standing behind you, nor do you have a Kingdom or civilization dependent on you. You are on your own. This makes achievement simple and difficult at the same time.

Water is the element of Chariot and so is it of Cancer. However, you will not find the presence of this element when you look at the Chariot card, it is imbued with deeper meaning. The warrior of the Chariot is a super sensitive, emotional and spiritual creature. Like its element, water, it is sensitive to every touch, drop or move but mighty and powerful enough to sweep out civilization if it wishes to. This is why you, as the warrior, wear the crown of stars, an indication of the heavenly connection between the body, mind and soul. You tend to be a diehard romantic and super sensitive. You can't be wearing your heart on your sleeve all the time, so you put up your guard to shield your heart from hurt and pain, which shows up as introversion, arrogance and reticence. Like you, the warrior tends to wear heavy armour to protect his heart but holds his head high in confidence and ruthlessness. Like the crab, which can live in and out of water on its terms, you too travel swiftly and with total ease in matters of the head and heart. Your spiritual wisdom makes you compassionate and an excellent judge of people, making it simpler for you to attain spiritual enlightenment.

Chariot is numbered seven after the seventh month of the year, July. Seven is also the number of spiritual wisdom and harmony. You are spiritual and love harmony. This is the reason why you have large families and big homes. Although you create this home single-handedly, you love the crowd of loved ones in it. One quality which connects you and Chariot strongly is your tenacity. The warrior is persistent in his goals. He is unshakeable and performs diligently to achieve his ambition. Your qualities reflect those of the Chariot. You can't function without your strengths and your strengths will be of no use without your command. You are tenacious and that is why you live in perfect harmony with your loved ones and yourself. You are a charmer and somebody who pleases others but on the flip side, this can make you a good manipulator.

Considering your hard exterior and high-handedness, you can become a bully and trouble people under you. You can be impulsive and impatient in the conquest of your goals, and this in turn could delay your achievements, causing unnecessary pain and stress. Your tenacity could drive away your partner, and make you arrogant and overbearing in other relationships too. There is a reason why you are so good with the knowledge of opposites, it is to help you maintain a balance between the good and dark side of your personality as in the two sphinxes of the Chariot. Put this strength to use and you will be victorious.

You have a lot waiting for you in 2019. This book will take you through the future through five different aspects: Monthly predictions, Love, Health, Wealth and Career. Enjoy knowing the unknown and put it to good use.

MONTHLY PREDICTIONS

JANUARY

The year starts off very well. I see a new readiness and willingness in you to accept love more openly, and initiate a new journey that will uplift your personal life. There is an onset of wealth. You will come up with some new ideas and thoughts that can lead to ways of wealth creation.

FEBRUARY

You need to take life a bit more easily and remember to have fun. Being tensed, anxious and always busy won't help. Take some time off, have fun and relax to make the most of your current position. Your work may be demanding this month where questions could be raised, and you would be under the radar of your seniors' scrutiny. Don't leave room for mistakes and put your best foot forward.

MARCH

A change is about to come this March. This change is positive and will set the course for new developments. Something must end for this new development to take place and this could cause some initial unease. You could face some discredit or defeat from your seniors, peers or people whom you are involved with. This is temporary and, in my opinion, you should simply go with the flow.

APRIL

This month is positive as I see you recovering from all the deficits so far. Whether it was wealth, money, health or love that seemed stagnated, it's all about to move in the right direction. A senior man, both in age and dominance, will help you out and guide you. You could also use discipline and better organizational skills to up your performance across all aspects.

MAY

You may be quick to pass judgements and jump to wrong conclusions. Avoid the tendency and evaluate all opportunities and decisions carefully. It isn't your problem if others are judgemental about you. You may shift houses or buy a new one this month. Marriage and happy events could also be on your cards this May.

JUNE

You are in complete control of your work. You will be moving forwards, spearheading projects and taking them to closure. This is great and, in fact, a woman will come to your aid. She is good at her work and helpful too. News of better job prospects is on its way to you. You will attract something better very soon.

JULY

You will complete whatever you had set out to do. Your goals and targets would be met, and this will bring forth important accomplishments. You deserve a pat on the back and must rest now. Perhaps give some thought to what lies ahead to better the situation. A predicament or difficulty lies ahead, and requires your complete attention and evaluation. A little isolation could offer clarity.

AUGUST

This is another fantastic month where wealth, health and happiness shall grace you. You shall do very well in matters of wealth and there is a possibility for marriage or childbirth during this period. There is gradual progress at work and you will be doing exceptionally well. Some good news and positive developments are coming through.

SEPTEMBER

A sudden change will occur this month. You could be expected to take a step back or compromise your own comfort. This may cause some initial teething issues and mental blocks but I advise to go with it, as the outcome would be worth the compromise. Your wealth will look good this month, you may be prompted to invest in renovating your home but take only as much debt as you can repay comfortably.

OCTOBER

A big confusion will cause a lot of anxiety this month. You have too many options to choose from. Make an informed decision as your future will depend on it. As we come to the end of the month you will have absolute clarity about what needs to be done next. You are ready to initiate a journey in life, especially in matters of the heart.

NOVEMBER

You will be buzzing with ideas and thoughts that could create more wealth. You are eager to put them into action and they will yield good results in all probability. You must remember to enjoy life amidst all these ambitions. Let your hair down and relax a little. It will motivate you to move ahead in life.

DECEMBER

A defeat is certain this month. You will feel discredited and disregarded. Your seniors and peers may be responsible for this. If you have become too negative in your thought pattern, now is the time to change that. A difficult and adamant man will influence your life this December. He cannot be toyed with, and you will have to find a way to deal with him.

LOVE PREDICTIONS

The predictions are divided into two parts in this chapter. The first paragraph will deal with the love life of committed Cancer and the next with that of the single Cancer.

JANUARY

You have to be patient for results in your love life. Be patient with your partner, and adapt a calm and composed demeanour. There will be situations this month where your patient approach will help you.

The single Cancer will see victory in pursuit of love. You will accomplish what you wanted in terms of an ideal partner.

FEBRUARY

Something is not right in your relationship. You two seem to be hurt and distant. There is some cause of worry which will bring you and your partner to two different ends of life. You may have to make some harsh, painful decision which, in my opinion, is the best for the two of you. You have done your best but the arrangement is failing anyway.

The Cancer who is seeking love will initiate a new journey. You may start something or take up an activity that will help you reach the ideal partner. You might just take the leap and consider marriage.

MARCH

You are feeling restricted and constrained in your relationship. You are not able to speak your mind or do what you want to. This is not a good spot to be in. You must have an open discussion with your partner about your concerns. Communication can ease a lot of tension.

The single Cancer will be ending something that can lead to positive developments. You are about to witness a change that will bring forth your heart's greatest desire.

APRIL

You will be making some progress in your relationship this month. Communication is clear and as needed. You and your partner will be making gradual progress, and initial troubles will begin to settle down.

The Cancer who is seeking love will have to take a break from the desperate search. You must take it easy and consider a holiday. You might just meet the perfect partner while you are on a break.

MAY

This is great month for the committed Cancer. You are in for happy times. I see both wealth and health gracing your family. You may be involved in large family gathering and happy events, which spreads love and rekindles the passion between you and your partner.

The single Cancer will face some difficulties this month. Not everything is as it seems to be. The castles that you built with expectations are all going to crumble.

JUNE

You need to take some time off and consider your options. Something is not right about your present situation. An old romance may have rekindled and you should consider if that is something you really want. Think it over and you will get your answer.

The single Cancer will meet an attractive and handsome man who will sweep them off their feet. The month is good and your prospects of love are bright.

JULY

You and your partner should consider taking help of a third person to resolve your problems. This person could be a counsellor or a guide who can hear you both out and present solutions.

The Cancer who is seeking love will come up with some bright new ideas to attract the perfect partner. You must act upon them quickly.

AUGUST

Your arrangement with your partner is about to come to an end or see some tough times, which could be caused either due to a decision to end it or because one of you may choose to relocate. This phase is going to be painful but it is needless to say that the decision must be made.

The single Cancer will be in a happy situation this month as your greatest wish in love is about to be granted.

SEPTEMBER

I see you involved in parties, anniversary functions or reunions, which will bring you and your partner closer. There is joy in your life, and these happy events will give you another opportunity to express love and affection.

The single Cancer needs to balance work and play. If you give too much emphasis to your career, how will you make time for love?

OCTOBER

There is a lot of stress in your life this month. The stress would be mostly work-related and might overwhelm you, making it difficult to manage your love life. Your love life will again go into a state of flux and you should consider making some time for your partner. Prioritize your love life!

The Cancer who is seeking love will find what he or she is looking for. You are about to get closure.

NOVEMBER

You have everything you need to make life comfortable, and I see you sharing this happiness with your partner. This month is great for your love life as I see you two very much in love.

The single Cancer should remember not to keep two swords in one sheath. If you are trying to consider two options for love at the same time then it is going to be a challenging task to perform. It's best to make a quick choice.

DECEMBER

You will learn a lesson about letting go this month. You must put the past behind you, and avoid being too clingy with your partner. You have a tendency of being fearful and holding onto people, which may cause suffocation in your love life. It's best to live and let live.

The single Cancer will end the year on a good note and I see you coming up with new and creative ideas to attract a lover who is just right. You need to act on them as soon as possible.

HEALTH PREDICTIONS

JANUARY

The year starts off brilliantly where I see you with a strong will to overcome any health issue that you could be facing. This month is great as it points to a strong line of recovery. Perhaps some discipline and consistency can render even better results. You will also receive aid from a man who is senior in both age and authority. He will help you in the healing process.

FEBRUARY

You are carrying too much baggage on your shoulders, and this is somewhat overwhelming you. You must learn to live in the moment and let go of what happened in the past. If you have repressed any negative emotions, you need to work on fixing this mental state. Introspection will bring a lot of clarity and peace. You could adopt traditional ways of healing and use the help of a traditional healer, such as an Ayurveda expert, or turn to a spiritualist or spiritual institutions. This may bring about the change you needed.

MARCH

You have a great deal to be proud of in matters of health. I see that you have done well, and are clear on what needs to be done to improve your present health conditions. Family events or functions will keep you busy and happy. In fact, the more time you spend with loved ones, the more you will heal internally.

APRIL

The news is not all good as I see an arrangement failing. You may decide to end a routine, treatment or therapy that failed to render results. This will take your hope away but ending it is the best option. You should also stay away from people who may be influencing your decisions negatively. Watch your choices and make informed decisions. Your lifestyle will also play an important role this April. Ask yourself if you have the tendency to give into your vices. If the answer is yes, then you know what must be done.

MAY

Your health could be at an all-time low due to feelings of sadness and defeat. You must continue your ongoing medications or routine. The situation will change for good and what you see now is only a temporary phase. As we come close to the end of the month, tarot would advise you to stay positive and hopeful. Hope is what will change your destiny in health; now is not the time to give up.

JUNE

There is an immediate need to balance your life. You may be juggling two important aspects of life, which may be stressing you out. Respite is on its way and as long as you can balance well, you will achieve stability in health. But some disappointing news will take you down emotionally. There is a negative revelation or news which will cause pain and discomfort. But only time can heal this so be patient with yourself.

JULY

You may be pushing yourself too hard too fast. Take it easy. Overdoing anything will lead to an injury and add to your health woes. It's best to enjoy what you are doing and go slow. You will receive positive news as we end this month. The news could be related to the results of some health tests you were expecting around this time.

AUGUST

You will be making gradual progress this month. Your health will begin to look up and positive results are on their way. Listen to your instincts and follow your intuition. If you feel something is not right with your health, then you should investigate the matter. It's always good to take a second opinion.

SEPTEMBER

You will meet someone important this month. This man will be determined and goal-oriented. He will help you achieve your health goals. On your part, you are ready to do what it takes to get where you want to be. The news that you are waiting for will come in due time. However, you may have to be patient.

OCTOBER

Work pressure is taking a toll on your health. There is more on your plate than you can handle. This seems to be overwhelming you. Take it easy before the stress gets to your health. The end of the month brings some respite as I see you settling down and situations beginning to improve. Your health will once again be restored to where it was before.

NOVEMBER

I see you are again doing more than what is needed. Give yourself a break and take it easy. Do only as much as you can and respect your body's limits. The month ends well with victory and conquest. You have done well and will see results for all the efforts you have put in.

DECEMBER

You need to be careful with whom you put your trust in regarding your health. Your health practitioner may be cheating you by ordering random tests. Watch where you are headed with him and do your share of research. A kind and sensitive woman will come to your aid. In fact, you will turn to your gentle and sensitive side, and reconnect with your feminine energies.

CAREER PREDICTIONS

JANUARY

The year starts off with celebrations and happy events. There will be reason for you to celebrate, such as some success you may have achieved, a reunion or an occasion. A highly influential and dominating woman is going to play an important role in your workplace. She can't be messed around with and you must handle her delicately.

FEBRUARY

You may be facing tough times as we step into February. There is too much to do and you don't know from where to start. You could be feeling defeated and may have reached a phase where you are considering fleeing. Hang in there, you have come too far and now is the time to stay put. Your boss or a senior will make work life complicated. But the best way is to not pick a fight or argument.

MARCH

You will come up with some bright new ideas and thoughts that can ease off a lot of work-related stress. These ideas have potential, and I see that you are ready to get them going and achieve your financial goals.

APRIL

You are at a point where you feel renewed, and excited about your career. There are some new developments that will keep you going and make work more appealing. If you are expecting news related to a job offer or a new opening, it's likely to get delayed. You may have to be more patient.

MAY

You will receive unexpected help from a senior. He is kind and gentle, and will offer you the best opportunity both in terms of remuneration and future career prospects. I see you starting something new. This is your dream project and if you apply all your skill and intellect, coupled with discipline and consistency, then success is certain.

JUNE

You will be in complete control of your work, delegating jobs and completing them as assigned. A woman be your ally and your team will render great results. However, you need to watch where you are headed mentally. There is some stress due to insecurity and apprehension, which may cause sleepless nights and unnecessary tension. What you fear is only in your mind. Don't pay heed to these negative thoughts.

JULY

Your work will be headed in the right direction. You will be making headway with your projects and assignments. Targets will be accomplished and there is a great deal to be proud of. You have done well and there is again a possibility that a woman ally will help you achieve one or more of these goals.

AUGUST

You will have to adopt a more traditional approach with work, at least that is what is expected of you. This may be difficult but it is doable. Your modern and unconventional ways may not work here. There is someone who is willing to guide you and help you through this patch. The month ends with some difficult news. Not all is what it appears to be. You may receive an unexpected blow as we come to the end of August.

SEPTEMBER

Beware of a man who may be difficult and judgemental about you and your performance. He is someone you can't trifle with but you will somehow have to keep his intervention minimal. You may step into people's ways while doing so and create some problems for yourself. Take it easy and respect others' space.

OCTOBER

You will reach a point of major confusion where a quick decision will have to be made. There are too many things going on in the background that will make this decision an impossible task. Beware of the fine print and take an informed decision. You will have a reason to cheer after all this tension as I see you happy and rejoicing in events that may be related to work.

NOVEMBER

Once again I see a feminine influence in your career. This woman may be someone you know personally or professionally. Her ideas and thoughts are diametrically opposite to yours. You must watch your back and keep her at bay. There are some ideas and thoughts of your own which can change your game plan for the good. You must work on them rather than depending on this woman.

DECEMBER

You will hear some positive news this month that shall set the course for better wealth prospects. You deserve every bit of this. Beware of people who could deceive and backstab you. This person cannot be trusted and I see you being discredited and feeling cheated. Practise vigilance to avoid this incident.

WEALTH PREDICTIONS

JANUARY

A financial arrangement will fail to render expected results and its closure is imperative. If this was your source of income then you will be in pain and face some deficit. The month ends well as you shall receive an unexpected bonus, wealth from ancestral property or family, winnings from lottery or an outcome of pure luck.

FEBRUARY

You are spending more than needed, and your vices and lifestyle are in dramatic contrast to your income. This is not a good sign and you will have to stop the spendthrift approach you have acquired. Use your money prudently as a big change is on its way. This change is great in terms of the final outcome but the initial blow will be hard, and your finances are likely to take a beating for a while.

MARCH

You will be on a break either from your job or from the source of income that forms the basis of your finances. This break will obviously cut off your flow of income, and you are advised to take it easy and use this time to think clearly. Whatever you are going through shall change if you exert your will in the right direction. Do not succumb to the situation and keep fighting as results will come.

APRIL

There is a need to balance your life and get more disciplined with your work. If your work forms the major source of your income then a disciplined approach will go a long way. During this time do not make any large investments and stay away from stocks. You must consider all financial openings and read the fine print carefully before you commit.

MAY

There is a delay in the news you have been so eagerly awaiting. This news could be related to returns on investments, income from work or better financial prospects. This delay may seem endless but being patient would be wise. The month may pose some financial difficulties where you will be at an all-time low financially. This phase is only temporary and you must stay positive.

JUNE

There is an immediate need to balance your income and expenses as the imbalance is causing a lot of financial woes. Take charge of where your money is going and how you are using it. However, one of your greatest financial wishes will come true by the end of the month. This could be a better job, a return on investment, a raise or a new home.

JULY

This month is fantastic, especially after all you have been through financially. You will be graced by the goddess of wealth who will bestow her blessing on you. There is prosperity and stability in your finances this month. In fact, tarot advises you to keep a positive attitude and stay hopeful for better outcomes.

AUGUST

You may be caught between two financial aspects this month. There is some amount of multitasking needed on your part to ensure both these elements stay that way. These could be two jobs, two investment avenues, etc. The end of the month poses a few challenges, you may be stressed about all those expenses that stand tall with your income falling short of them.

SEPTEMBER

The low income phase is once again history as September brings forth abundance and prosperity. Your hands will be filled with the best that money can buy as I see your times changing. You must continue to attract these positive outcomes; after all, wealth is all about a mindset. Stay positive and hopeful and you will see positive returns.

OCTOBER

You will be caught in some kind of a confusion that may take a toll on your wealth. You must make a quick, informed decision which has the power to influence your overall financial status. This situation may be stressful but it needs your attention. Beware of cheats and liars who may siphon money from you. You must not put your trust in people who are capable of deceit. Be vigilant as theft could take place.

NOVEMBER

A caring and loving woman will play an important role in shaping your finances. Listen to her advice carefully and follow her instructions, she will guide you out of your woes. By the end of the month you will be in complete control of your finances and would be moving in the right direction after all.

DECEMBER

You will initiate something new in matters of wealth such as a business venture, a new job or a new investment avenue. This is great considering its potential but remember to factor in the risks involved. This new initiative is adventurous and rewarding, and I am sure you will enjoy it thoroughly. But if you are looking at doing two things at a time like managing two jobs or two financial avenues then it is best to pick one to minimize risks and increase gains.

Leo – Strength

23 July–22 August

ॡ

In tarot, the card that describes you goes beyond in explaining the essence of your existence and creation. You are the Strength card in tarot and there is a purpose to your being called that. As far as the title goes, it is a card well associated with Leo, at least for its name. You have the strength and the vigour of the lion.

The Strength card from the Rider-Waite tarot deck has a female angel dressed in a white robe, wearing a crown and a belt of flowers. She has a symbol of infinity over her head and is shown taming a lion. The lion submits to her kindness. She is fearless and poised. There is no aggression on her face or in her actions. The card is yellow with a blue mountain in the background. Now let me make this simple for you.

In the Strength card, you are both the lion and the angel. The lion represents your innate desires, and the angel your power to keep these desires in check. The lion represents you on a physical plane; the angel represents your mental and spiritual power. This implies that you have the mental strength to overcome your physical nature. You have the strength to overcome any odds, physical or mental, because you are blessed with inner strength. The card's yellow colour stands for prosperity and balance between the conscious and subconscious, mind over matter. The crown and the belt, made of natural elements, represent the beautiful earthly creation that you are and your earthly purpose of realization. The infinity sign symbolizes spiritual power, thus completing the trilogy of Body, Mind and Soul. You are by far the only sign that has so much control and power over yourself that external factors can rarely shake you. This is the true essence of the Strength card, strong and powerful inside. Look within, my dear Leo, and you will know what I am talking about.

Leo is powerful yet modest. You are the majestic lion on the outside and a humble servant within; you are a true combination of outer and inner strength. These qualities go a long way in making you a great companion. People look up to you for the strength you exhibit. They depend on you for good kingship and you are able to meet this expectation very well. You have a big heart, and tend to forgive and forget easily. Grudges don't go with you to the grave and all this is because of the strong sense of self that you have. You are like the woman in the card taming the wild beast, an impossible thing to do but one you manage with grace, you make the lion your pet. You have the valour to fight the impossible and accomplish tasks with ease. No conflicts, no hurt, no pain can overtake you; you tame them all. This makes you a happy, ferocious and mighty beast. This is why you are always centre stage and why people love you.

You play various roles in life with complete ease and poise. The combination of inner and outer strength makes you enviable. As a partner you are trustworthy and loyal. You love to rule; whether it's your home, your friend circle or, for that matter, your spouse. You are misunderstood for you rarely fight for domination; domination and authority is given to you. Your partner readily submits to your charm and love. This submission is like the lion's to the angel. You are the alpha in any relationship.

On the flip side, you can be pompous and bossy and this can sometimes make relationships difficult. Your powerful charisma can overshadow your partner. As a friend, you are fun to be with. You take to adventures and crazy stuff easily. You love to be at the front like the lion, and care about the ones behind you. You move in prides and will therefore always have a large family and friend circle. You want to keep everyone together but this can be annoying if pushed beyond a point. You have to agree to not have your say always, which doesn't go down well with you. You can be melodramatic and dominating to make things go your way. This may drive people away. As a parent, you are a fabulous and fun person to be with. Your child will look forward to spending time with you and learning to ape your styles. But your over-protectiveness and overbearing interference in this child's life can ruin your relationship. Eventually it is all a matter of will; you have the will to overcome these weaknesses and harness only your strengths.

You are a lethal weapon made to strike the right target to turn good from bad. Your spirit is strong and your ultimate purpose is realization, which you can achieve with ease if you put your mind to it.

Fire is the element of the Strength card. Fire denotes vigour, vitality, energy and aggression. These are the primary characteristics which make you passionate and fiery. The Strength card is numbered eight, implying the eighth month of the year, August, which is also the month of Leo.

The number eight represents balance and that's perfect for the Leo in the Strength card. All you do is strike a balance between your inner and outer self. You are realistic, practical and intelligent; the qualities of a person belonging to number eight whose constant endeavour is to use his or her inner strengths to fight the odds outside. All the aspects of your zodiac fit in perfectly with the description of the Strength card. I hope you have enjoyed knowing yourself through tarot.

As Strength, you have a lot waiting for you in 2019. This book will take you through the future through five different aspects: Monthly predictions, Love, Health, Wealth and Career. I hope this book serves you as a clear guideline to what lies ahead.

MONTHLY PREDICTIONS

JANUARY

This month is good as I see wealth coming in. You will be at the peak of your health too, and may consider starting something of your own like a small business or a new work project. This month will comprise of good omens like marriage, childbirth, prosperity and good health.

FEBRUARY

You are on the brink of action in your career. Work should be looking good, and an authoritative senior man will take a liking to your work. There is accomplishment in the goals you wish to achieve. You will succeed against all odds and come out victorious.

MARCH

There is an imbalance in your life that requires immediate correction. You are either overdoing something or ignoring other important elements of life. This will cause some stress. It is important you take a closer look at the way you are conducting your life and make changes. You may face defeat at the hands of co-workers and seniors who will discredit you, and brand your work as theirs. This is going to be a difficult phase but picking fights is not advisable.

APRIL

You will receive a sudden setback this April. The news is not good and what comes forward will bring your dream castle crumbling down. What is revealed has been going on in the background for some time now. After this event, you will reach a point where it will be easy to pass the blame onto others, but tarot advises you to look inwards and figure out the problem.

MAY

You will meet the perfect person you have been looking for. In fact, what comes forth this month is a manifestation of your wishes. You may have yearned for love, wealth, health or a better job. Your wish is granted and your passion comes to life in May. Your work begins to pick up and there is a great deal to be proud of. You have done well and earned every bit of success that comes.

JUNE

An arrangement may have to be closed as it renders futile. This could be related to your personal or professional life. You have to move on and moving on requires letting go of something dear. This will cause pain but is ultimately a good decision. You will take a walk down memory lane and meet someone or something that will rekindle past memories, but use this opportunity to create a meaningful present.

JULY

You are confused and your predicament needs a lot of thought. There is a problem at hand which needs your undivided attention and sole judgement. Do not listen to others; introspect for a while and the answers will come forward. This is not the time to make risky decisions without thorough evaluation.

AUGUST

You will meet a woman who will influence your decisions this month. She may have always been around or is someone who has come along later. She is strong-willed and highly opinionated. You must keep her intervention minimal. Use your creativity and sensitive nature to create something unimaginable. Your love life will be on an upswing this month.

SEPTEMBER

You may consult or meet someone senior who will guide you and help you through your concerns. This may be a senior in a professional setup, a counsellor or a spiritual institution. The month ends well where I see an unexpected sum of money coming in as a result of family income or pure luck. You may also be involved in large family events like marriage as we end this month.

OCTOBER

You are ready to explore life and love. There are certain ideas and thoughts in your mind which have the power to shape your destiny. You are thrilled and eagerly looking forward to a new beginning. A man, someone you know or work with, will act as an impediment in your progress. He is not on your side and you must deal with him gently.

NOVEMBER

You should take it easy and learn to enjoy life. You are stressed and losing out on all the fun life has to offer. Make some time to relax and do the things you love. Situations get tense as we approach the end of the month. You have to choose from many options and this seems confusing. Take your time and research your options well.

DECEMBER

You will be making gradual but steady progress in your life. Your work will be moving in the right direction. You may be travelling within domestic boundaries to complete your work assignments. Look out for the mental stress that comes along towards the end of December. You may feel cornered, defeated and lost. Something is not right about your workplace but giving up now may not be a good idea.

LOVE PREDICTIONS

Your love predictions are divided into parts. The first paragraph will discuss the love life of the committed Leo and the next will talk about the single Leo's love life.

JANUARY

Your relationship has witnessed some tough times lately but as you step into the new year, things will begin to improve. Your love life will recover from the issues and will have sailed through the rockiest patch. You are now on a more settled turf.

The single Leo will start something new in order to find the perfect match. You have all it takes to attract the right person; you only need to believe.

FEBRUARY

You may tie the knot this month and get hitched for life. Marriage, childbirth or even official engagement, and commitment is on the cards. You are in for some happy times ahead.

If you are looking for love, then this month is great as I see you moving in the right direction to achieve your goal.

MARCH

This month is great and will give you many reasons to be happy. Your partner has the same feelings towards you as you have for him or her. There is love, understanding and chemistry in your relationship.

The single Leo will start up something new like a vocation course or class that will put them out in a forum where they can attract a desirable partner.

APRIL

Your love life will be witnessing some happy times. All the effort you have put in will pay off. You will get your desired outcome and there is stability in your love life this April.

The single Leo will take a look in the past and come upon a person or memory that will open the door to opportunities in love.

MAY

This month will pose some challenges as you begin to question your partner's contribution and external factors that you believe are influencing your relationship negatively. You must look within and before question yourself before you blame others.

The single Leo will have to get over the past in order to make something happen in the present. What had occurred is history, the present is a gift.

JUNE

You will once again be at a crossroads where you will question your partner's intention and contribution. Before you pass the blame, check if you are doing your bit to keep the peace and love intact in your relationship. Some introspection will bring clarity.

The single Leo is going to be swept off their feet by an attractive, intelligent and charming character. Be ready for the joy ride.

JULY

Your relationship will be back on track and you will both share love and understanding. There is affection and maturity in your relationship that comes after dealing with the difficulties life poses.

If you are seeking love, beware of reaching a point of desperation. Stay calm and focused. Avoid desperate thoughts as you may eventually attract what you think.

AUGUST

You will initiate a new beginning in love. This may mean formalizing your relationship through an official commitment like marriage or engagement. You have apprehensive about this but trust your instincts; it's a risk well planned.

The single Leo will be at a point in life where a big change will set the course for new beginnings. This change will get you what your heart yearns for.

SEPTEMBER

Romance will be going rather well. You may resort to some old-fashioned ways of expressing love and conducting the affairs of the heart. It's good to try something new and different.

If you are looking for a partner then September is the month to put your new ideas into action. Do as your mind wants you to.

OCTOBER

You are in for some happy times where just about everything is going right in your relationship. You will have an abundance of love and joy. This is the time to thank the universe for the blessing of a true loving companion.

If you are single then adopting some traditional methods of seeking a partner will greatly help you. Look at old-fashioned channels; they have the answer to your pleas.

NOVEMBER

Drama is about to unfold. Something is not as right as you expected it to be. A revelation may cause pain and hurt. You should try to stay strong as that's the only way to deal with this difficulty.

The single Leo will meet someone genuine, sincere and kind. This person understands love and values relationships.

DECEMBER

If you are stuck in a difficult relationship and are in it only for the security it offers, then it's about time you made a decision. You can't keep brushing your problems under the carpet. However, if you choose to stay in your relationship then accept this as a decision for life.

The single Leo will face some difficulties as their plans may not go as expected. You may feel disappointed or defeated.

HEALTH PREDICTIONS

JANUARY

Your health will be looking good as you start the year. You have a great deal to be proud of; especially all the efforts and discipline that you put in to reach where you are now. The month ends well and I see a new enthusiasm in you to improve your health routine to maintain the fitness levels you have achieved so far.

FEBRUARY

You will receive some financial aid if that is what you need to reach your health goals. This will help you get the medical intervention you need. There is a need to balance your life. Take a close look at your schedule and see if you are missing the balance by overdoing or not doing something in particular at all.

MARCH

You will meet a traditional healer like an Ayurveda specialist or a spiritualist. His intervention would heal you at much deeper levels. Your work may pose some challenges and this will bring about increased stress levels. Watch your health during this time as the situation isn't all that good. Do not give up on your routine medications or treatment; stay consistent.

APRIL

A partnership is about to be initiated in matters related to health. This may be a new routine like going to the gym, doing yoga or anything that helps achieve your health goals. I see stability and good health for you this April.

MAY

You will come up with some brilliant ideas to stay motivated and active. Put these ideas into action and see the wonderful outcome it yields. But your mind will play games with you and cause unwanted stress. You are insecure about something which leads to apprehension and worries. The thumb rule to live a happy and balanced life is to stay positive. Think about it!

JUNE

Your health will look good as you start this month. I see you involved in happy events with loved ones which will boost your emotional well-being. If you are expecting test results or outcomes of any health investigation, it is going to be delayed. The results will come when the time is right.

JULY

Your test results or some revelations shall arrive which will not be good. You may be in for some trying times, so be careful about how you conduct your health. Perhaps a good break or an international trip would help. This may add excitement to your life and give you some well-deserved rest.

AUGUST

There is an imbalance in your life that is causing a lot of mental pressure. You may be torn between two opposing factors of life and the sooner you correct this imbalance the better it is for you. The month will end well and you will be rewarded for your consistency and discipline. You will be back on track with your health looking good.

SEPTEMBER

There is definite recovery from whatever you were suffering so far. You will achieve conquest against all odds and come out victorious. This is due to your will to fight and courage to overcome your fears. A kind, loving and sensitive man will positively influence your health this month. You should consider turning to your creative, sensitive side to draw out a renewed perception on life.

OCTOBER

You may face some emotional difficulties this month. Health will not be at its peak and there is some emotional unrest. Before you blame external factors for this, you must look within and try to find the answers to your questions. The right mental attitude will greatly help. The good news is that I see you recovering from this phase and getting back to a stable, happy and positive state of mind.

NOVEMBER

Tarot advises you to stay hopeful and positive. There may be many problems and issues but a strong heart can overcome anything if it truly believes in good and happy times. You must stay focused on your goals and trust the universe as success is not far. You may face a small disappointment as November ends. Heartache and emotional turbulence may set in again but this is only a temporary phase.

DECEMBER

There is an imbalance that needs to be corrected immediately. Ensure that your fitness regime is on track along with your medications and other aspects of health. Sleep well, eat right and remember to meditate for a peaceful state of mind. The year ends with a break for introspection. You may reach a point where some clarity in life would help greatly and there is no better place to seek this clarity but from within.

CAREER PREDICTIONS

JANUARY

The year starts very well where a woman will become your ally and help you achieve work targets. Your work will be in full swing and appreciation, recognition and rewards are in store for you. In fact, you may walk away with a bonus or a satisfactory increment of some sort as the month ends.

FEBRUARY

You are juggling between two bosses or two kinds of jobs. This may make work life a little difficult to balance but there is very little you can do except multitask. Respite will soon come if you stay focused and continue to juggle the two elements well. The month will end with a dream coming true. If you were waiting for the right job, assignment or raise, then it is likely to show up this month.

MARCH

You will be stuck at a crossroads where the dilemma is very serious and needs immediate attention. You will be confused as there will be too many options to choose from. Take your time and make an informed decision. You will finally choose to start something of your own like a new venture or business start-up. This is great considering your potential and interest.

APRIL

You are happy and comfortable with your job. There is a lot to look forward to and thank the universe for. I see one of your greatest wishes coming to life this month. There are certain risks and important steps that need to be taken. You must follow your instincts and listen to the voice that is guiding you from within. Go with what you strongly believe in.

MAY

Your work performance will be much better this May. The difficult times have settled and you have made it safely to the shore of stability and comfort. Avoid making hasty decisions and judgements about others. If people are judging you then that's purely their problem.

JUNE

You are in total control of the work assigned to you this month. You are clear about your strategies and are working diligently on putting them into action. Success is guaranteed after such efforts and I see you achieving your goals easily.

JULY

Owing to the last month's success, I see you making merry and raising a toast to success in either a reunion or an office gathering. This is the perfect time to celebrate and spread the cheer. You will earn good profits or income for what you have done and recognition and success comes along with it.

AUGUST

You will be at a peak in your career where prosperity and success will grace you abundantly. You may get a hefty bonus, increment or an offer with an impressive pay cheque. You are moving upwards in your career graph where there is lot of domestic travel involved as well as a great deal of networking exposure.

SEPTEMBER

You will be starting a new vocation, class or course that will help you achieve the best in your career. This will add a lot of value to your ongoing job or will help you get a good break. If you feel stuck in a job or detest what you do, now is a good time to make a firm decision and bring about some change. If you choose to stay where you are, then own up to the decision and stay happy.

OCTOBER

You will choose to end something that leads to a new beginning. This may mean either calling it quits or changing your course of actions for a better opportunity. Doing so will definitely bring forth the transformation you desire and lead to new ideas and thoughts that could change your destiny if acted upon.

NOVEMBER

You may feel deceived or cheated at work this month. Watch your back and stay vigilant about how your peers and seniors, treat your work and performance. Stay on your guard and do not trust people easily. The sudden negativity will restrict you and feelings of defeat and apprehension will prevail. But speak up when needed and express your intentions clearly.

DECEMBER

You must move on from what might have occurred some time ago. If you are insecure about something then you are likely to hold onto things that would hardly matter otherwise. Let go of all these insecurities and negativity. Let the energy of life flow through you. The year ends with some amount of introspection where you begin to blame external factors for your issues. It would be wise to take a look at your own self to understand if you have done your part well.

WEALTH PREDICTIONS

JANUARY

Your wealth will have a good start this year as you may initiate a new vocation or job that helps you improve your financial position. This is good and is likely to add value to your current status. You shall receive good news on your wealth prospects in the next few days. This may be a new business assignment, a job offer or an investment opportunity.

FEBRUARY

You will be facing some difficult times this February. Money flow would be tight and this will lead to some sacrifices and compromises that one has to make when income is scarce. Look at it positively, this situation will help you get to a better place soon. Accept the change that has come and you will see a positive outcome in time. Your finances will look better as you approach the end of the month.

MARCH

You may buy an automobile such as a car or a bike. This is good and denotes good stability of wealth. However, do not spend more than you need to as times ahead will once again pose some financial difficulties. You may hit an all-time low after this large purchase but this phase is temporary.

APRIL

You will be making gradual progress in your wealth. This is good as what is slow will last longer. There is some positive news coming along this April. It may be related to your work and shall open the door to opportunities for better wealth stability.

MAY

You may be tempted to overspend or use money inappropriately. It will be wise to use your money prudently. Avoid unnecessary expenses and do not give into temptation. A big change is about to come and start a new journey in your life. This change will greatly impact your finances.

JUNE

There is stark recovery in your finances this month. If you were struggling with money issues then June is when you will see light of day. You will begin to see situations move in your favour and bring forth stability in wealth. You may undertake overseas travel for either leisure or work and this break is well-deserved.

JULY

You may be going after an assignment or work opportunity that is promising but competitive. There are lot of takers for this but you stand a good chance. The month ends well with a great deal to be proud of. Your finances will be better and you will have absolute clarity about what needs to be done next.

AUGUST

You will be happy and on a positive frequency which will attract bright opportunities. You are filled with an enthusiasm to do something new that will lead to more money and stabilize your finances. This is great and you should act upon it. You will receive financial aid this month from someone senior to you. This aid was much-needed and will help you transform your current financial position.

SEPTEMBER

Times are about to change for the good as I see the wheel of fortune turning in your favour. You will see unexpected positive developments which will lead to better wealth opportunities. You are in for some surprises that will transform your life. A woman shall come to your aid and your work is likely to be responsible for these positive changes.

OCTOBER

You must overcome the sadness or guilt of the past and make the most of the present. Do not waste time over what has already happened. It is time to stop brooding and take charge of what lies before you – a sea of opportunity. You may see contracts or legal agreements fall into place this month. You just need to pay close attention to maintaining balance in your finances.

NOVEMBER

You are in for some happy times. You may buy a house or move places this November. Happy events like marriage and engagements are on your cards. This only goes to say that your finances are stable and growing. You may be juggling two wealth opportunities at this time. Continue to balance them as that's the way to glory and success.

DECEMBER

Your finances or investments may take a beating this month. Something is not right and a small setback is on your cards. This may leave you feeling disappointed but don't waste time over it. The good news is that, in spite of all the deficit, you will still recover and fight back to achieve conquest. Victory is certain and you will end the year on a good note where wealth and success will both grace you.

Virgo – Hermit
23 August–22 September

♍

Life's journey for a Virgo can be challenging as you are not limited to the material world alone. You are intrinsically inclined to derive more from life, especially spirituality and wisdom. Material success, wealth and other goals complement you but doing the impossible, like achieving the knowledge of another dimension, defines you. According to the tarot card associated with your zodiac sign, you are a very spiritual person; you are the sceptic, the sage, the wisdom. You are the enlightened one, and hence you have the onus of showing others the way. This can be an overwhelming responsibility, and yes, my dear Virgo, this is what your life is all about in tarot – a beautiful spiritual discovery of yourself and others. Your tarot card is Hermit; a sacred and interesting card. Now, you may say, 'I am anything but spiritual!' Well, if that's so, your journey of self-discovery hasn't yet begun and I am glad I will be the one to open the gate to this journey for you. Come, let's get to know the real you, the Hermit in you.

The Hermit card in the Rider-Waite tarot deck has an old man; he is the wise sage or the Hermit walking in search of something on snow-clad mountains. He wears a greyish-white robe, has a beard, holds a staff and carries a lantern to light the way ahead. The lantern is lit up with what seems to be a six-pointed star in it, which is Solomon's seal of wisdom. The grey cloak indicates the secrecy of his achievements and work, visible only to the few whom he believes are worthy of it. The snow-clad mountains represent his attainment of spiritualism, wisdom and knowledge. The staff in his left hand, which is connected to the subconscious, represents authority and power over his kind of world; a world that he has discovered through his mysterious journey of self-exploration. In simple terms, the old sage represents knowledge gathered by him in his isolation, knowledge that he is ready to share with others. He walks on a path trying to discover more about himself through the understanding of life as a spiritual journey. The sage is shown in constant movement; this implies constant growth of wisdom and knowledge. The card is numbered nine, which stands for completion and accomplishment of goals or ambitions. It also symbolizes the ninth month of the year, September, the month of Virgo.

How on earth are you like the sage? Good question. I know it's difficult to relate yourself with a sage, or yogi as you may like to call him, so let's take it one step at a time. The pictorial representation of the Hermit card shows a sage who is on the move, not sitting or hiding. You are a person who often thinks analytically, gathering information and analysing situations. You are restless to find the cause of any problem or situation; just like the Hermit constantly seems to be looking for something. Your approach of giving attention to every detail makes you a critical thinker like the sage. You are the kind of person who will go out in the dark with a lantern to explore what's going on, a true sceptic, and will do just about anything to rest your doubts and questions. Your curiosity leads you to explore the deepest secrets and unravel the darkest mysteries. You have a keen sense of responsibility towards others which compels you to share what you have learnt with your loved ones. You therefore make for a fantastic teacher, therapist or mentor. You are patient, kind and wise; you are the agony aunt of your group. People love you because you are the calmest of all, poised at all times and can give unbiased judgement like a sage. You pick and choose your confidantes and friends, and most often appear to be reticent and shy, but that is just the cloak of secrecy you wear.

You never leave a task unfinished and do whatever it takes to complete it. That's typical of you, you are a logical and analytical thinker, a person who will look into every detail meticulously and evaluate the options for the right decision. This comes from the Hermit's experience of thinking logically in complete isolation before arriving at a conclusion. If you come across a problem, your first action is to isolate and introspect. You think before you act. You like living in harmony in large families and will always strive to be harmonious with others.

The element which rules the Hermit card is earth. You are modest and humble like the Hermit in all possible ways. This makes you a great worker who is authoritative and modest at the same time. Your attention to detail is an asset to your workplace or, for that matter, anywhere you have been put to work. As a person, you are loved by all. You fit in perfectly well in various roles of society. You are a loving parent, a patient teacher, a helpful and reliable friend, an understanding lover and an efficient worker. Nowhere do you stagnate. In every walk of your life, in every role that you play, in every assignment that you undertake, your Hermit sensitivity is evident. I love this tag, the Silent Hermit! I hope you have enjoyed knowing yourself through tarot.

As the Hermit, you have a lot waiting for you in 2019. This book will take you through the future through five different aspects: Love, Health, Wealth, Career and Monthly predictions. I hope this book serves you as a clear guideline to what lies ahead.

MONTHLY PREDICTIONS

JANUARY

You will be making a lot of progress in your personal life as we start 2019. If you are single, there is a positive chance you will find someone heart-warming and loving. Your work may go through some stressful times. You may have to secure your position and will have to handle a lot of pressure and tension to do so. Do not give up what you are working on as success is near.

FEBRUARY

You may be stuck between two opposing elements that pose a lot of challenges. Two different people, jobs, bosses or situations are pulling you apart. You have to correct this imbalance soon or you will need to take drastic measures. Pay attention to your work performance. You are being watched and your work is under scrutiny. This is not the time to falter, so put your best foot forward.

MARCH

You will be buzzing with ideas and thoughts that can lead to wealth-making opportunities. You should act on these ideas as they have potential. There is also a readiness in you to do what it takes to turn the wealth chakra in your favour. However, at the emotional front, an arrangement might have to end to make way for better prospects. You may consider relocation or a change for the better.

APRIL

Your work is about to undergo a new beginning. You are ready to take on something exciting and this brings a great deal of enthusiasm in you. March is a good start for better career prospects. It is important you bear in mind that whatever the case may be, you should not give up your dream or your hope. Now is the time to hold on to your dream as it will soon become a reality for you.

MAY

You may take a break for a short period. This break may be important for putting life into perspective or for health reasons. In either case, it will serve you well and do what's needed. After this break, I see you renewed and charged to take on what lies ahead bravely. You are clear about your work and sorted about what kind of opportunities are best suited for your skillset.

JUNE

A small theft or robbery may take place this month. There is also a possibility of someone backstabbing or deceiving you. Stay vigilant and be on your guard. Do not trust people easily. The good news is that in spite of all your adversaries, you will quickly recover from the incidents. Your health will look especially good this month.

JULY

You may travel overseas or take up opportunities abroad. This travel could be either for work or pleasure. There is also a possibility of childbirth. There is happiness and prosperity in store for you this month and this time would serve you even better if you were to let go of all your insecurities, baggage and feelings of remorse and guilt. Do not hold on to what is not yours, even money and power. Let go and more shall come your way.

AUGUST

Your work will be on an upswing this August. You are in charge and in complete control of your work assignments or targets. Everything is going smoothly and there is a possibility that a woman ally will aid you in achieving this. Your love life is about to witness a new beginning as I see you ready to do what is needed.

SEPTEMBER

If you are looking for a job then be forewarned about the stiff competition out there. There are formidable opponents for the position you seek. Your chances are good if you choose to play fairly. In matters of the heart, you may initiate a new affair or a short-lived partnership that has good prospects.

OCTOBER

Good news related to wealth and health is coming this October. You may receive an unexpected sum of money from an ancestral property or your family income. This could also be wealth from lottery or similar sources where luck plays an important role.

NOVEMBER

You will be facing am emotionally turbulent time this November. Your love life and emotional well-being are going to be tested. There may be a lot of emotional upheaval and tension which can cause stress leading to depression, sadness and anxiety. You must maintain your mental balance at all costs. There is an important decision that needs immediate attention and good thought.

DECEMBER

You are creating a lot of negativity by harnessing negative ideas, insecurities, apprehension and tension. Let them all go. These negativities are causing sleepless nights and will take a toll on your health. Most of these issues don't even exist and are purely a figment of your imagination. The best way to fix these issues is to figure out ways to balance the opposite elements that you are caught between at the moment. Try various combinations and you shall succeed in striking the right balance.

LOVE PREDICTIONS

Your love predictions are divided into two parts: the first paragraph will address the committed Virgo and the next para will discuss the future of the single Virgo.

JANUARY

The year starts off well with stability in your relationship. There is mutual trust, respect and understanding. If there were difficulties in the past, this month marks recovery from all of that.

The single Virgo will face stiff competition to get the one he or she desires. There are either too many takers for your prospective lover or for you.

FEBRUARY

This is a good month again where everything seems too good to be true. But truth it is, your relationship is perfect and it's time you thank the universe for this gift.

You are going to meet a headstrong and charming prospect if you are seeking love, but this person will have a tendency to overshadow you. So know what you are getting into before you leap.

MARCH

If there were issues in your love life then this month you shall witness some recovery and stability. All that was difficult is over, and you will be in a much better and happier state this month. This was possible only because of your will to withstand all the odds and turn the situation to your advantage.

The single Virgo will meet someone sweet, kind and sensitive this month. This prospect is very positive and you could definitely make something good out of it.

APRIL

Your relationship will be complete with all that you wanted in it. There is nothing more that you could ask for and you should count your blessings.

If you are looking for love then you must take life a bit easy. You are becoming anxious and troubled about love prospects, and now is the time to live in the moment and enjoy every minute that goes by.

MAY

You are ready to express emotions of love more openly and do what is needed to keep your love life happy and smooth. Your partner will reciprocate in a similar fashion and appreciate your expressions of love.

The single Virgo will receive rewards for the efforts they have put in to find a good partner. You are in for some happy times this May.

JUNE

You will be working on new ways and ideas to bring about a positive change in your relationship. You must act upon these ideas as they have potential.

The single Virgo will be facing feelings of loneliness and sadness. You may be left alone whilst others seem to find true love. But you too will find the right partner in time.

JULY

One of you is being dishonest to the other in this relationship. It is always advisable to be transparent, and encourage lucid communication. Be more receptive of your partner's problems and hear him or her out clearly. If you are being discreet about something, know the consequences of such discretion.

The single Virgo is about to see times changing for the good. You are ready to meet the one you seek so desperately.

AUGUST

You may be passing wrong judgements or making hasty decisions around this time in matters of the heart. If you have such a tendency, slow it down and think before you speak your mind.

If you are seeking love then this month indicates the need to act on all those ideas in your head that you believe can lead to a good partner.

SEPTEMBER

Either of you will be taking complete charge of your relationship and shaping it in a manner which is conducive to a stress-free life. There is also a strong influence of a demanding professional life this month. Prioritize your life well.

The single Virgo will be meeting a knight in shining armour. Get ready to be swept off your feet.

OCTOBER

You will initiate new ways to maintain the peace and stability in your relationship. Whatever you plan to do is easily within your limits to achieve. You have all it takes to make this initiative viable.

If you are looking for love then a kind, lovable and approachable person will step into your life this month. This could lead to something lasting if you work on it.

NOVEMBER

Conflicts and arguments are likely to occur this month. You must hold your ground and handle matters assertively but not aggressively. You could be overstepping the mark with your partner and therefore it's important to listen before you comment.

The single Virgo will have to pay attention to the present and get over the tendency to look into the past. You must forget what was or what happened and live in the moment.

DECEMBER

You will be moving forward in your search for a stable, happy relationship. You are blessed with a good love life and I see that you two will work together to make your home a more comfortable place to live in.

The single Virgo will end the year by undertaking a new vocation or class which will put you out in a forum of potential lovers. You need to be in a place where you can meet the right candidate and this is just the right start.

HEALTH PREDICTIONS

JANUARY

Your health looks positive as we start the year. You are happy and content with your achievements in health so far, and have a lot to be proud of. Give yourself a pat on the back and try to multitask the two routines you are currently involved in. Give priority to both health and other aspects of life, and do not compromise on the former.

FEBRUARY

You may hear some positive news related to conception, marriage or childbirth. This is great and you must now focus on your complete well-being. You will be doing very well as I see you on the brink of a lot of good events taking place around you. There is reason to celebrate and cheer but avoid binging.

MARCH

You will be taking the necessary steps to fix your health issues if you have any. You need to be disciplined and driven to accomplish the resolutions you have set, and that is exactly what you will be doing this March. You may consider ending something that failed to work and this will bother you. The idea of ending something comfortable to follow your heart's call will cause some amount of apprehension, stress and worry.

APRIL

You will start something new this month that will make you enthusiastic and excited. You are eager to prove yourself and you must immediately act on this idea to improve your health. This month will mark a sudden and positive recovery in your health. You will begin to settle down and see some positive and healthy times ahead.

MAY

You must take everything with a pinch of salt at this juncture regarding your health. If you feel the tests or treatment your doctors are advising isn't right then seek an alternate opinion and get to the bottom of it. This is the time when you should follow your intuition. If you feel something isn't right then work on putting your doubts to rest. The month ends well and there is recovery and well-being.

JUNE

You will be doing exceptionally well this month as far as your health goes. This is the month of the genie, where you can make a wish and it shall be granted. Ask and it will be given! You may have to bring about a few lifestyle changes for longevity, and greater stability in health. Eat right, exercise well, sleep well and meditate once in a while. This will render long-term results.

JULY

You will start a new health course, routine, treatment or regime which will be focused on getting better results. This is good and will help you achieve the desired outcomes. Perhaps if you balanced your life a little more your health woes would get fixed. Take a closer look to find out what you are not doing right. These small changes can yield good results.

AUGUST

You must learn to let go of the past for your overall well-being. The longer you hold on to past grudges, guilt, sadness and failure, the longer you will be rejecting your present good. Learn to drop the baggage and move on. Unfortunately, an event unravels this month that brings your dream castle crumbling down. This revelation will cause anxiety and stress. You must stay strong to deal with it and this too shall pass.

SEPTEMBER

Your emotional health will be much better than what it was last month. You are more stable and ready to take up the challenges that come next. You are eager and willing to make the necessary changes and work the situation out accordingly. You will receive aid from a healer or doctor who is quite senior to you in age. This help will go a long way in fixing your health issues.

OCTOBER

You must take a closer look at your lifestyle. If there is an imbalance then work things out before it is too late. Tarot advises you to keep your addictions, vices and indulgences in check this month. You may end up paying a big price if you overindulge or give into your weaker side. Be careful about how you conduct yourself.

NOVEMBER

A change is needed and shall come forth in November. You must change your attitude towards your body and mind. Keep your stress levels in check, and avoid alcohol or any sort of intoxicants. This change shall set the course for something new and promising. If you observe discipline, you will attain a huge transformation. This is also the time to listen to what your mind and heart tell you and do as they suggest.

DECEMBER

The year ends brilliantly where I see you happy and settled with your loved ones. This is the time when you should thank the universe for the gifts it has bestowed on you. Relationships are one of the most important gifts, and you will have them all. A woman shall play an important role in your life this month. She is caring and sensitive; listen to her and follow her guidelines.

CAREER PREDICTIONS

JANUARY

Your problems will begin to settle down at the workplace. As you step into the year, work will look better and there are signs of improvement. You will undertake domestic travel and receive networking opportunities offering better exposure.

FEBRUARY

The situation this month seems tough as an important decision has to be made. You are confused between too many options and do not know which to choose. A wrong decision can land you into trouble, and you must watch where you are headed. As you end the month, you may have to make a choice to end an arrangement that is failing to yield results in spite of your repeated attempts to revive it.

MARCH

You will meet someone or something from the past to help you connect the dots. There is a possibility that an opportunity may work out due to this. There are no coincidences. Your work will be going well this March, and there is recognition and rewards in store for you. You will be enjoying all that comes with a stable, secure job.

APRIL

If you are expecting a job offer or news of better prospects then it is likely to get delayed. You will receive the news when the time is right; stay patient until then. In the meanwhile, don't turn against yourself, your beliefs and restricting thoughts could be an obstacle in your own progress. You may also be feeling constrained and restricted from freely doing what you wish to. You must break free and speak up when needed.

MAY

You will choose to take a short break. This break will give you some time to think clearly and understand your priorities. After this break you will have absolute clarity about what needs to be done next in your career. Your choices and decisions will be rather clear with clearly defined career goals.

JUNE

You have to be patient to get to where you want to be. If you are expecting a raise, promotion or bonus then know that it's on its way. Don't get restless and adopt desperate measures. You may start a new vocation or course that will help you achieve more from your career. This is good, considering the potential of the vocation you have chosen.

JULY

A man, senior in both age and authority, will come to your aid. He will guide you through all the difficulties in your workplace. He is someone who prefers a methodological, organized and disciplined manner of working. You should adhere to these standards in order to work closely with this person. If you begin to get obsessed about job security and apprehensions start bothering you, calm down and learn to let go of all this tension. They will only create an obstruction in progress.

AUGUST

You will fail to end an arrangement that wasn't working out. Some aspect of your career is not functioning right and its end is definite. You will have to make some tough decisions, considering the situation that arises this August. You may have to resort to some traditional and conventional ways for working out the problems. This change in perspective will help immensely. Consulting someone knowledgeable will also help.

SEPTEMBER

You will be making slow but consistent progress in your career this month. The situation is likely to improve and things will go as planned. You may also receive some positive news. There is a renewed excitement and thrill in your approach towards work. I see that you will be geared and charged to accomplish your targets, and will do exceptionally well in meeting them on time.

OCTOBER

Beware of deceit and treachery. Watch your back and don't trust people easily. There is a possibility of someone lying to you or disregarding your work. Stay cautious but avoid jumping to quick conclusions or making hasty decisions. It is always advisable to make an informed decision. Your work will be under scrutiny so don't leave any room for errors.

NOVEMBER

A contact from past will come forth this month. You will get nostalgic and take a walk down memory lane. This is great, considering the opportunity and clarity you will receive from this past acquaintance. Your work will be on an upswing and you will achieve all that you expected from it.

DECEMBER

You shall receive what you are expecting with some delay. This may be related to a new job offer, a work assignment, etc. You will get what you desire when the time is right. You may decide to take a break towards the end of the year, either for leisure or health reasons. This break will serve you well, as you shall attain complete clarity about your career choices and other important decisions related to work.

WEALTH PREDICTIONS

JANUARY

The month begins with the need for some restraint and caution. You must be careful with where you choose to put your money. Use your wealth prudently and avoid making risky decisions. Do not trust people or investment avenues blindly, and if you find something suspicious, try to get to the bottom of it. The month ends well where I see you undertaking international travel and making the most of what money can buy. This is an indication that the risky phase has ended.

FEBRUARY

Cash flow will be tight this month. Most of this situation is due to your attitude towards money. If you continue to allow feelings of scarcity and lack then you shall attract the same. Adopt a wealthy mindset to attract wealth and give more if you want to get more. The month ends with some negative news or an event that will surface suddenly and bring your dream castle crumbling down. Stay strong and be patient.

MARCH

You will initiate a new venture which will lead to more wealth and better financial opportunities. This set-up will need your belief more than anything to make it work. This month is very positive as the wheels of fortune turn in your favour. Times will change for the good and most things that seemed difficult will move smoothly.

APRIL

Last month's positive events will lead to even better outcomes this April. You will be churning ideas and putting your thoughts to work, leading to greater wealth opportunities. These ideas have potential and you must act on them quickly. The month ends with your recovery and a total reversal of your deficits. Your finances will gradually begin to be restored to normalcy.

MAY

You will be making gradual and steady progress this month. Good news may be coming your way. This month is more stable but emotionally stressful. Your wealth will be on an upswing and there will be a lot to look forward to.

JUNE

It's important to stay positive and hopeful, and that's exactly what tarot advises you to be. Do not give up on your dream and continue to work towards it. You may be caught at a crossroads where an important decision will have to be made. There are too many options to choose from but you must research and make an informed decision.

JULY

A financial arrangement is about to fail and see its end. You have done everything in your capacity to save it but closing this avenue is the only way out of the present situation. This decision may be painful but it is needed. A past acquaintance or memory shall open the way to better wealth prospects.

AUGUST

Beware of theft, robbery or deceit. Someone is not being entirely honest to you. Make informed decisions and do not trust people easily. You may enter into a partnership-like arrangement towards the end of the month which promises good rewards.

SEPTEMBER

Some negative news or revelation is about to come forth this month and will greatly impact your finances. You may reach an all-time low. But after the downfall, rise is the only option; therefore, you will rise to greater heights of wealth stability by manifesting one of your dearest financial wish.

OCTOBER

You will meet a man who is opinionated and difficult to deal with. You may have to work with him as his contribution is imperative to your financial stability this month. You shall see victory against all odds. Your work will look good, which is indirectly responsible for your wealth stability.

NOVEMBER

You may buy an automobile. This indicates your finances are improving but beware of unscrupulous characters who may lie to you or steal from you once again. It's better to take precautions than remedy the situation. Be forewarned and stay vigilant.

DECEMBER

You will be happy and content with what has come about financially this year. You will choose to look at the glass as half-full rather than half-empty. There may be some tension around managing finances. Use your money prudently and don't get overwhelmed, you will eventually find your way through this. Restrain yourself from indulging in large expenses and use money where it is needed most.

Libra – Justice
23 September–22 October

♎

You are the Scales in zodiac. Scales denote equilibrium and balance. This is by far the most essential quality common to your zodiac and the card that describes you in tarot. As an individual you are just and balanced like the Justice card, your card in tarot. As the name suggests, you are all about justice. It is a heavy word, it sounds overwhelming, as though shouldering a huge responsibility. In all honesty, you do.

The card in the Rider-Waite deck has the Angel of Justice sitting on her throne wearing a red robe and a golden crown with a square gem. There are two pillars on either side of her throne. In her right hand, she holds a double-edged sword pointed upwards and, in the other, a scale in a state of perfect balance. There is a purple curtain or veil in the background. The card is numbered eleven. The angel here is you, the figure that enforces law and order. I don't mean law in literal terms but the laws of the universe and nature. The female form of the angel denotes your sensitivity and kindness of heart. These two qualities are associated with women, and hence the angel's form highlights your predominant characteristics. Her crown stands for knowledge and the power to govern and pass judgement. You have the gift of genius and intellect, the crown that you wear, that you use to make right decisions in your life. The double-edged sword denotes impartiality and the direction it points to represents victory. You are impartial and fair most of the time, which is why karma favours you and guarantees victory to you. The purple veil represents the spiritual world, which is an important part of your physical existence. The red robe stands for authority and the power to make or enforce laws and maintain balance. The pillars on either side denote the good and the bad – the angel and the devil. You have a thorough understanding of the good and the bad in your life. You never lose sight of this understanding and are therefore logical and practical. The scales that you hold in your left hand, the hand of the subconscious and intuitive mind, stand for equilibrium; the sole purpose of your life. Balance is the essence of the Justice card and it is what you are here to do.

The number eleven on your card signifies genius and good communication skills. This is why you are such an articulate and intelligent speaker, one who hardly ever goes wrong with words. This is also because of your ruling element, air. Air denotes excellent communication skills that make you a great charmer. The angel's sole aim is to establish equilibrium in life, and so is yours. If at any point in time you lose your sense of balance, you will do everything it takes to restore the calm and equilibrium in your life. You try to strike balance at home by being a good parent and laying the foundations of rules and regulations that you encourage with love and compassion. At work, you seem to be the fairest of all. You are an excellent boss as you are unbiased and just to all. You make for a great companion too. You are kind, compassionate and loving; someone who won't waste time fighting. In fact, you love to do things in pairs, in coordination. You love company and are a lovable and stable partner. You are a supersensitive individual with the brain of a genius. This makes you a great friend and a hard taskmaster in your field of expertise at work. Overall, you are an excellent individual.

Your greatest strengths are your sense of fairness and your quest for harmony and peace. This makes life interesting and challenging at the same time. You are diplomatic too, after all, you have the double-edged sword of genius and intellect which makes you a smart talker. These qualities, when used correctly, inspire equilibrium and balance in life – give and take, love and be loved, win and lose – turning you into an angel. When these qualities are deployed for selfish and dark gains, you can be as dangerous as the devil, as overbearing and over-protective as a parent, and as dishonest and treacherous as a worker who leads by wrong example, spreading wrong work ethics. As a lover, you may get too insecure and possessive due to your overwhelming sensitivity, which may suffocate your partner and drive away happiness from your relationships. You could be a self-obsessed friend who thinks of only personal gains at the cost of others. Spiritually, you may be a liar who destroys the karmic balance of the universe with fake practices and dark dogmatic rules. It is thus of paramount importance that you establish balance in both aspects of life, the good and the bad. You are a good person with the potential to go bad.

As Justice, you have a lot waiting for you in 2019. This book will take you through the future through five different aspects: Monthly predictions, Love, Health, Wealth and Career. I hope this book serves you as a clear guideline to what lies ahead.

MONTHLY PREDICTIONS

JANUARY

The year starts very well for you, especially in work and matters of the heart. You will receive a positive sign when it comes to your love life that shall set the course for new and exciting developments. More importantly, your work should also take a turn for the good. You may receive good news regarding job offers or new work assignments. Make the most of this time and don't take life too seriously.

FEBRUARY

A big change is about to come and sweep you off your feet. You may see the end of something, only to make way for a transformation that awaits. All the pain, hurt and difficulties are about to end for a new beginning. I see that you may start a new initiative, like an organization or a venture, that is fresh in ideas and thoughts. This venture has the potential to succeed as long as you believe in it.

MARCH

You will meet someone caring and loving this March. This person is willing to express love and go out of his or her way to accommodate you. If you are already in a relationship, your life shall be witnessing some happy times in March. But don't let boredom ruin the thrill. If you are bored with something, work out ways to rekindle the spark and revive the passion. Blaming others is not an option.

APRIL

There is some tension and emotional upheaval that will cause issues in the beginning of the month. You must watch the way you conduct your personal life, especially your love life. There may be conflicts and worries which could drive you nuts. Be calm, don't make hasty decisions and, if needed, talk to a counsellor who can guide you through troubling times. It's best to consider some alone time as introspection can lead to answers.

MAY

You will come up with some ideas and thoughts that can take a lot of burden off your shoulders. You must act upon them immediately. I see you choosing to end an association or something that wasn't yielding results. This decision may be hurtful but it's important you do it.

JUNE

You will be victorious this month and work will be on an upswing. Recognition, rewards and victory are all yours. You are at an all-new spot where reaching was difficult but maintaining the position will be even more challenging. You will achieve your heart's greatest desire as we exit this month. You are in for some happy times!

JULY

Cash flow and finances may be low as we start this month. You are thinking of scarcity and, therefore, will continue to attract deficiency in wealth. You need to give more to get more! If you have repressed emotions, address them. There is an imbalance in your life that you must correct by observing the various aspects as you may be ignoring something important.

AUGUST

One must work hard and make important changes to achieve something. You may have to bring about some drastic changes which may include taking a step backwards to move forward in life. Some compromises, occasionally, will render positive results. A wise person is a part of your life this month who may step in as a counsellor, spiritualist or healer.

SEPTEMBER

Your work looks good this month. You will be delegating and ensuring the targets or assignments give the best results. An authoritative and senior man will aid you in this task. Life is good and relationships and family will play an important role. You have a lot to thank the universe for and now is the time to do so.

OCTOBER

A new journey is about to begin. This is related to an initiative you will undertake this October. It is different, adventurous and challenging. I see a lot of good coming out of this, if you stay hopeful, focused and positive.

NOVEMBER

You will start a new vocation, course or class where I see you unlearning to learn new skills. This is a good decision as what you learn will help you in the future. The month ends with celebrations and parties where there is merrymaking and fun. You could be part of a reunion, birthday bash or anniversary celebrations that give reason to have fun.

DECEMBER

The wheel of fortune will turn in your favour, there is a clear indication that wealth will grace you and prosperity is at hand. The year ends perfectly where money, good health, love, marriage and even news of childbirth is a possibility.

LOVE PREDICTIONS

These predictions are divided into two parts. The first will address the love life of the committed Libra and the next will discuss the predictions of the single Libra.

JANUARY

You will adopt old traditional ways of rekindling the spark in your love life. This is a great approach and it may work wonderfully. You could also consider taking to someone about your issues or conflicts and getting a third person to intermediate your differences, if any.

The single Libra will recover from all the problems and be ready to look at life with a renewed perspective. You are in the right frame of mind to get to where you want to be in love.

FEBRUARY

You will come up with some interesting ideas to better in your relationship. You may also decide to put an end to something you disagree with in the relationship.

The Libra who is seeking love will achieve something important this month. Conquest in love is definite this February.

MARCH

Your relationship will be going well as you step into March. You have lot to look forward to and all the credit for coming this far goes entirely to you. You have worked hard to achieve stability and peace in your love life, and truly deserve a pat on the back for this.

The single Libra must devise various ways and means to make love happen. There is an imbalance in your life due to which love is being compromised. You must correct this imbalance if love is a priority.

APRIL

You are living in the past this month. Regrets, guilt or memories are holding you back. You must move on and forget what happened. Focus on the present as that's where you and your partner stand today. The success of your relationship will entirely depend on your efforts in the present moment.

The Libra who is looking for love will meet someone from the past and a series of events will unfold. This blast from the past will rekindle romance and could lead to the lover you were awaiting.

MAY

You are ready to make changes and work out ways to make your relationship work. Putting these ideas and thoughts in action is important. You are goal-oriented and will be working hard to achieve stability and success in your love life.

The single Libra will be focusing too much on work, leaving no time for love. You must balance your life if love is truly a priority.

JUNE

You may face some disappointments in love this June. Not all expectations or commitments will be met by your partner, and life may leave you feeling dejected and sad. It is best to forget and move on to maintain your happiness.

The Libra who is seeking love is too overwhelmed with work pressure and professional commitments. If you continue to focus on work this extensively then the other aspects of life like love are going to be compromised.

JULY

Mild conflicts and communication problems will arise. It's good to know when to push a point of view and when to back off. Sometimes it is good to let go for the sake of avoiding an argument. You should also respect your partner's space.

The single Libra will try out traditional ways of attracting the one they are interested in. These old ways and methods will prove to be useful.

AUGUST

Patience is a virtue that will be most useful this August. You must deal with your partner gently and patiently. Don't get restless and aggressive. You will see results of your patience if you wait it out and give your partner some time to adjust to the situation.

The Libra who is looking for love will come up with new ideas and thoughts to attract a prospective partner. These ideas and thoughts are only useful if you act upon them.

SEPTEMBER

There is a major imbalance in your relationship this September. You and your partner are going in two opposite directions where synergy is impossible; but success is possible if you try. Keep trying to strike a balance by involving your partner.

The single Libra will make good progress in matters of the heart as you will meet someone interesting and exciting this month.

OCTOBER

You may meet someone from your past or come upon something that reminds you of old times. This chance meeting will bring back a lot of good memories and rekindle the spark. If you happen to meet your ex now, be forewarned about passion emerging between the two of you. Know where you are headed with something like this.

The single Libra is about to witness a more settled and happy phase where love will be easier to attract, and a potential lover is very much within reach.

NOVEMBER

You need to strike balance in your life. Your professional life is taking over everything and you are too involved in your career to give time to your lover. This may be the beginning of a long-term problem if you don't resolve it at the earliest.

The single Libra is about to be swept off his or her feet by someone charming and attractive. You are in for a joyride.

DECEMBER

Your work is once again taxing your brain. With all the mounting work pressure, tension in personal life will also increase. You are mixing your work and personal life without any demarcation at all. You must set your priorities before love gets pushed into the background.

If you are looking for love, then this month is going to be a slightly challenging one. You may find yourself lonely where everyone else is with someone they love. This phase is temporary and you will see good times soon if you stay hopeful and positive.

HEALTH PREDICTIONS

JANUARY

You will take a walk down memory lane which will bring back happy thoughts and memories. Your past will play an important role in reviving health and fitness. You may chance upon an object, material or person who will boost your health indirectly. But results can be achieved only if you are willing to make a few sacrifices. Cut back on things that you are overdoing and see a life-transforming outcome.

FEBRUARY

You are going strong in the fitness quotient. You will be working hard on your health goals but it is always advisable to go slow and make steady progress. Don't injure yourself by overdoing it. Times ahead are about to change. Your health will only get better and luck will play an important role.

MARCH

You may receive good news of conception or childbirth in March. The month starts well with good health and happiness, but as you move along, you may begin to have feelings of withdrawal caused by a negative thought pattern. This is also the time when your health may suddenly dip and situations could get a bit hazy.

APRIL

You will take charge of your health and fitness and begin to move forward. If there are some ideas and thoughts in your mind, then it's best to act upon them immediately. This prompt action will render good results. Your recovery will be speedy and you will see good results this month. Where there is a will, there is a way and thus you shall get results after the efforts you have put in.

MAY

You will be at the peak of your health and happiness, fitness and prosperity will grace you. There is a lot to look forward to and thank the universe for. You will also undertake a partnership with another person for better health and improved fitness.

JUNE

If you are expecting test results, then they are likely to get delayed. You must be patient, they will come soon enough. Don't get restless and continue to work towards better health. You will be juggling two important health treatments, regimes or even health and work. Multitasking would be a challenge initially but soon you will cope with it.

JULY

You will be feeling good and healthy this month. There is a lot to look forward to. An adamant and well-read person will be part of your health scene. He could appear in the capacity of a healer or someone who greatly influences you. But you must know what is wrong and right for yourself, and make a well-informed decision instead of simply going with the flow.

AUGUST

You could be jumping to conclusions and making hasty decisions. It is important to consider the consequences before you take a leap. Go slow and avoid hasty decisions. There is a certain amount of mental upheaval and trauma. Don't let any symptom go unnoticed and seek help immediately.

SEPTEMBER

Your health will be back on track and family functions and happy events will keep you busy. The love and prayers of loved ones will get you back on your feet. A certain problem may cause some tension. This is about a decision which needs to be made and requires a lot of introspection. Take some time off and be alone to seek out the answers. You will realize you have been overwhelming yourself and causing unwanted health issues.

OCTOBER

There is a lot of hope soon. Stay on the plan you are working on and don't give up. Results will come in due course if you stay positive and hopeful. There is victory this October. You shall achieve conquest and accomplishment in the you have targets assigned to yourself in matters of health.

NOVEMBER

There is a need for change. This change in perception, attitude or lifestyle can greatly transform you. One such change shall come forth and end all your health woes. You may find it difficult to deal with it initially but you will begin to see results as time goes by. Positive outcomes and results are definite towards the end of the month, and this was only possible because you worked so hard on it.

DECEMBER

As the year is about to end, you need to also take it slow and easy. Do not overdo any activity and enjoy what you are doing without expecting quick results. It's also good to take it easy and live in the moment. You will be caught in a confusion where a choice must be made regarding matters concerning health. Weigh the options carefully before you settle with a decision.

CAREER PREDICTIONS

JANUARY

The year starts with caution. You must beware of treachery and deception. Someone will deceive you and betray your trust. There is also a possibility that your credit could be stolen by someone else. But the month ends on a good note. You will be involved in celebration, parties, reunions, etc. which will bring cheer and joy.

FEBRUARY

You will receive good news this month regarding a job offer, a new profile or an assignment that seems promising. A compromise must be made to fit into what lies ahead. You may have to accept a pay cut or take up something which is slightly lower than what you are currently doing. Accepting this change could be difficult but can lead to a positive transformation.

MARCH

You will be surprised with the sudden turn of events. I see you receiving a surprise bonus, incentive or raise. You will be happy with the way situations have turned out. You will also undertake domestic travel and be right in the middle of action. This is a good opportunity to learn and network.

APRIL

You are at the right place and at the right time. This month in tarot is called the month of the genie. If you ask for something, it shall be granted. Your career will be on an upswing and flourishing. In fact, you are just about to get into a partnership or a joint assignment that will yield good returns.

MAY

You must pay close attention to work performance and not leave any room for error. You are being watched and your work is under scrutiny. This is not the time to falter, instead, put your best foot forward and hold your ground. The good news is that by the end of the month you will receive due credit for the work performed and tasks achieved.

JUNE

You will be at a crossroads where an important decision must be made. The decision pertains to a choice that may become increasingly difficult to make as time passes. Evaluate the options well and weigh the consequences before you make a decision. An influential and interfering woman is a part of your work scene. You must know where to limit her intervention and watch your back.

JULY

The month doesn't start too well and some bad news may come forth. This may seem like the end of everything, and lead to a strong feeling of defeat and loss. But time will heal and bring about change. You need to stay strong and focused. Events after this seem positive as I see a new window of opportunity opening that can lead to a fulfilling career.

AUGUST

You will decide to close an ongoing association to fulfil your dream. This may mean the end of your existing work set-up or a relocation that promises better opportunities. Although painful, this decision must be made. Situations get tough as we progress towards the end of the month as both money and work opportunities seem scarce. You may feel left out and abandoned when others walk away with a good raise, bonus or appraisal.

SEPTEMBER

You will be doing well this month as work picks up and there is gradual progress. You could also receive good news regarding better prospects. A strong and dominating man is going to be a part of your work scene this September. He may be your immediate boss or a colleague and you should deal with him diplomatically.

OCTOBER

Don't get tempted to make quick decisions and pass wrong judgements. Be patient with work and people around you. If others are judging you then it is their problem, not yours, you must focus on your work and performance. Do not give into the mental negativity that is harming your sleep. Your sleepless nights are the outcome of apprehension and insecurity. Keep negative thoughts at bay.

NOVEMBER

November is the month of accomplishment. You will complete all the tasks or targets assigned to you. This will lead to feelings of accomplishment and conquest. But do look out for what lies ahead. You may end an ongoing work association because of the lack of results. This may be a project, job or association which you thought wasn't leading anywhere. Although tough, this decision was much-needed.

DECEMBER

Your work is going to get challenging as we start December. You may be harnessing feelings of defeat, loss and fear that will cause you to surrender and give up everything. Tarot advises you to stay on as success is near if you withstand the test. Opportunities will come if you are looking for a job but competition is stiff. You must play fairly and give your best to get to where you want to be.

WEALTH PREDICTIONS

JANUARY

The year starts great where I see the wheel of fortune turning in your favour. This implies lady luck and fate shall both grace you. Your financial situation is about to change for the good and there are some pleasant surprises planned. There is a lot of good waiting for you this year; you must stay hopeful and keep moving forward in your goals to achieve wealth.

FEBRUARY

A big change will come in and set a new course of events into action. This change will end something and lead to a new beginning. This sudden end will affect your finances greatly. The month ends with a new initiative that paves the way for wealth and money. You will start something that seems very promising.

MARCH

You will taste victory this March and most of your financial woes will seem like history. You are invincible and will achieve a great deal of success in your investments. You may consider purchasing an automobile. There is more to come as I see wealth from ancestral or family sources making way to you.

APRIL

You shall receive good news which will emotionally uplift you and give you a brilliant breakthrough to expand your financial portfolio. There is absolute clarity about what you must do in matters of work and investment. You are ready to set course for a new path.

MAY

You will receive a good bonus, an impressive raise or a promising incentive. You are cash-rich and have reason to celebrate. This might just be the time to launch the business you have been thinking of. You are on an upswing on wealth graph where money will be consistent, and there is gradual but definite progress.

JUNE

You will be churning new ideas to make money, and success is definite if these are acted upon. You could achieve the impossible if you feel like it, but insecurities fear and apprehension might get the better of you and turn you into a negative storehouse. You seem to end the month worried, with fears of lack and scarcity.

JULY

An intelligent and articulate man is going to influence your finances this month. However, it is advisable to be careful and apply your own logic to his advice. Make decisions carefully and use thorough vigilance. Your finances will reach a stage of completion this July where one or more investment avenues will mature, rendering good results.

AUGUST

If you are awaiting some news related to wealth or finances, then it is likely to get delayed. You will get what you are waiting for in due time, but patience is important until then. You might be in a competitive state where your finances will depend on your job or on some other opportunity. You will get what you seek; just stay focused and play fairly.

SEPTEMBER

You will receive good news this September, which will bring you a reason to be happy and joyous as it opens a window of opportunity to make money. However, getting restless won't help. You must be patient for the results of the investment. If you are expecting returns, then stay calm and be patient.

OCTOBER

You may face a small disappointment or sadness this month. Something isn't right. A commitment made to you may not be fulfilled or some promise will fail to meet its end. This will cause rejection. Your money in the market may not perform well. The good news is you shall receive financial aid from a well-wisher.

NOVEMBER

You must use your creativity to crack some interesting ideas that can lead to better prospects. A sensitive, smart and creative woman will guide you. Follow her guidance and you will see the tables turn. The end of the month is going to be a challenging period where money will be scarce, and you may reach an all-time low in finances. Stay positive and things will definitely change.

DECEMBER

You will receive good news that will uplift your spirits and put you back in the game again. There is reason to cheer as the year ends with absolute clarity workwise and promising opportunities that can lead to better financial stability.

Scorpio – Death
23 October–21 November

♏

You can be best described as the stinging, poisonous scorpion on one hand and the peace-loving, gentle dove on the other. This is going to be very exciting for you, my dear Scorpio, I can assure you that. Your journey in tarot means a new beginning. You always make a fresh start from wherever and whatever you have been doing.

The card that is associated with you may sound a little scary and spooky but that only goes to show the intensity of your sign. You are the invincible Death card in tarot. Wait a minute, do not jump to conclusions before you have read this chapter thoroughly. Death is just your card; at no point does it imply the end of your life. Relax! You need not worry or fret because it is Death that marks your entry in tarot. It is as intriguing and exciting as the concept of death. I would love to take you through all the questions buzzing in your head right now. Why the Death card? How does it relate to you? What is your position in tarot if you are the Death? Let us take one step at a time. I will first explain the physical implication of the card and then interpret it in relation to you. As I describe each aspect of your card you will have to keep your focus entirely on the picture of the Death card. Look at it carefully and absorb its details.

In the card, you will see Death riding a horse. Death is denoted by the skeleton's head to which the armour is attached. Death carries a black flag with a white flower on it. There are three characters paying homage to Death – a man dressed like a pope, a woman and a child. The background is grey. The horse that Death rides is white and it seems to be trampling over someone who looks like a prince.

The sun, far in the background, seems to be setting between two pillars. The card is numbered thirteen.

Now let's simplify the above. Death in the card wears an armour and shield, which imply how invincible and unconquerable it is. It rides a white horse, which represents purity of purpose. It is out there to do what it has to; nothing can change that and no one can stop it. It will come when it is time. The three characters of man, woman and child paying homage to death imply that death is impartial, be it a man, a woman or a child. When it comes, it comes with the purpose of doing its job, as it has been depicted in the card by Death's horse trampling over a corpse, irrespective of the person, rich or poor. The black flag denotes the end, the white flower a new beginning. The sun in the background represents immortality – it sets to rise again, a kind of rebirth, a transformation. The two pillars stand for the good and the bad of the Universe. The grey background denotes the unbiased and impartial judgement of Death.

The Number thirteen on the card denotes destruction, end, rebirth and transformation, a new and promising beginning. The Death card stands for change – an end only for a new beginning to come. It is hence a very positive card which you need not fear. In fact, it is one of the mightiest of the cards and you should feel lucky to be associated with it. The common thread between you and the Death card is the concept of transformation, I'll explain how. Scorpio is about metamorphosis, changing from one form to another to adapt to its surroundings.

You are a Scorpion to start with: once you have mastered the art of dealing with the poisonous tail, you transform into the Eagle which sweeps its prey off the ground with the precision of a hunter; lastly, you settle into the form of a Dove. Each of these three stages depict the following cycles of your life: you start with learning about the self, then master your skills and use them well, and finally take to renunciation for peace and spirituality. This is the transformation that you, as a Scorpio, undergo and this is what defines you. The Death card too does the same. It is about change, transformation and rebirth.

All this fits in perfectly with your metamorphosis. You are indeed an intense sign that bears the qualities of adaptation to suit your everchanging life. This is what I love the most about you. You are comfortable in your skin while going through these transitions. You're incredible – intense, passionate and ever-changing. You are a passionate individual who changes for no one but your own self. You can rise, fall and rise again with complete ease. You most often learn from your mistakes rather than regret them. You love change and can easily adapt to it. You are a loner simply because you are in absolute peace with yourself; you don't need constant companionship to enjoy life. You adapt well to changing scenarios and make life fun for you and others. Most importantly, you are a mysterious person – a riddle that most of us would love to unravel. This makes you very attractive to the opposite sex. Your secrecy and ever-changing attitudes of tempting, and persuading keep your love life passionate and exciting, making you the unpredictable lover. Then again, you can change into an overbearing lover driven by insecurity, and too much secrecy when transparency is needed. There is always a flip side to you. No one except you knows what you will be.

As a parent, you are fun at once but difficult at other times. You can be easy-going and intrusive at the same time. Your child often finds it difficult to interpret your parental behaviour. Again, you are most loved because of this dynamic personality. Your child therefore looks forward to both a great friend in you and a protective guide. As a worker, you are a genius, an asset and a gifted individual, but jealousy and pride can get the better of you. You can be difficult and aggressive with your subordinates. They may not understand you since you wear this veil of an ever-changing person.

You are by far invincible because of your genius and your unbiased judgement, which makes you a terrific asset at work. You are the unconquerable 'death' from the Death card; the mightiest of all to whom each and every one bows. You are indeed both the head and the tail of a coin as you can adapt to being either at your own will. This explanation should be sufficient to begin your journey in tarot. I am sure this has intrigued you, trust me, it only gets better as you dwell into the unseen 2019.

As Death, you have a lot waiting for you in 2019. This book will take you through the future through five different aspects: Monthly predictions, Love, Health, Wealth and Career. I hope this book serves you as a clear guideline to what lies ahead.

MONTHLY PREDICTIONS

JANUARY

You will be at the top of your game in your professional life. Work will be looking good with tasks and targets being achieved. You will turn into a kind of task master, spearheading projects and enjoying the power that comes with this responsibility. A woman will aid you in this success. The month ends well with rewards and recognition coming in. You may also consider home shifts, a house purchase, marriage or moving in with your partner to start a new life.

FEBRUARY

You will be receiving some good news this month. The news is about wealth, prosperity, marriage and childbirth. You are in for some happy times ahead. The new beginning and positive developments lead to happy thoughts and ideas which, if worked upon, can lead to better prospects. You should also consider enjoying your life and soaking in the present moment for a bit.

MARCH

You will be ready to start afresh. This is the time when you must let your hair down and enjoy the happiest moments of life. Don't take life too seriously and consider falling in love or at least getting ready to take that leap in matters of the heart. You may end this month with a slight bitterness, where a heart break or disappointment causes pain and hurt. But this phase is only temporary.

APRIL

You will choose to end an ongoing association which fails to work out. This could be in your professional or personal life. You have done your bit and it may just be the right decision to move on. You could be expecting news related to work, which, in all probability, is likely to get delayed.

MAY

Your professional life would be demanding in terms of time and attention. There are going to be some tough times ahead where you must remain calm and focused. This is not the time to err. The good news is the times ahead are about to change for good. You will get lucky and things will begin to move in your favour.

JUNE

You must learn to relax, take it easy and enjoy the space that you are in. If you are being too aggressive or pushing too hard, then slow down. There is no need to do that as it won't render results. If you are expecting news, then it will come but may not be all that positive. You should learn to balance your life, there is something amiss in the way you are conducting it. Correct the imbalance and choose a side.

JULY

You will receive good news of better prospects or a financial breakthrough. This is great and you must immediately capitalize on this opportunity. You could also receive the financial aid you have been looking for from a source which is kind and giving. This will greatly help you in financial matters.

AUGUST

You will be making haste and may take wrong decisions or pass wrong judgements. Slow down and do what you must by avoiding hasty and wrongful decisions. Be patient and situations will turn in your favour. Your personal life will be at its best this month and there is much to thank the universe for.

SEPTEMBER

You will be doing very well this month financially. There is a big bonus coming your way. You may also consider starting a new venture or business. You are about to receive good news related to work and better work prospects. This is such a fabulous month!

OCTOBER

You may be a bit confused and hassled about your current problem. There is something that bothers you and it requires your complete attention to detail. You should consider some alone time to introspect, and a solution will surface. You are all set to start the big new venture and, trust me, you have all it takes to succeed. You need to believe in yourself and in the venture. Go for it!

NOVEMBER

You must learn to have some fun and experience the good things of life; enjoy the space you are in and don't take life too seriously. Simply have fun! This month is just right for that considering all the good things that will come through like wealth, health, marriage and even news regarding childbirth or conception.

DECEMBER

You are about to meet someone exciting who will sweep you off the feet. You are happy and content with life. Love will blossom and there is a lot to look forward to. Manage your work pressure because that is something that may overwhelm you; take on your plate only as much as you can eat. Keep work stress at bay and meditate once in a while.

LOVE PREDICTIONS

These predictions are divided into two parts. The first paragraph addresses the love life of the committed Scorpio and the latter of the single Scorpio.

JANUARY

You may be feeling loveless and bored as you step into the year. Your relationship may have lost the spark, and you are wondering if help could come and fix the current situation. If you look closely, you may realize that you hold the key to happiness. Sometimes it's best to check within before you blame others for a problem.

The single Scorpio will be involved in family functions and such other events which could lead to a prospective partner.

FEBRUARY

You are feeling left-out and lonely. This may be the result of unresolved inner tensions that lead to negative thoughts. You must communicate your feelings to your partner and resolve inner conflicts. Don't let it go unnoticed till you erupt sooner or later.

The Scorpio who is seeking love will find a good match this month. This person is strong, authoritative and a task master. You must play carefully and know how to handle such a strong character.

MARCH

You will hit the wall and end something that wasn't working out. A big change will sweep you off and lead to a new transformation. This may imply an end of the relationship that you are in or something difficult about to occur that sets the course for a new beginning.

The single Scorpio must not act out of desperation. You should be patient and learn new ways of attracting a good partner. Desperation will only create problems for you.

APRIL

A new and adventurous beginning waits this month. You may decide to get committed or take a leap of faith in marriage. This is great and will come with its own set of thrills and apprehensions. But the decision is good from where I see it and should lead to an exciting new journey ahead.

The single Scorpio will have an exciting month ahead where you will be noticed by other potential partners and you may just meet the right person.

MAY

You will choose to take a break with your partner and spend some quality time together. This is a good initiative as it will bring you two closer and help rebuild the bond.

The Scorpio who is seeking love will start something new and challenging. This is the right place or medium that could connect you with the perfect companion.

JUNE

You will sail through the difficulties and will arrive at a much better position in your love life. This month is more stable and peaceful when it comes to your relationship. There will be a calm that comes from your understanding and love for each other.

The single Scorpio will have to make some changes in his or her lifestyle to get to where they want to be in love. You are unwilling to do this and therefore may feel stuck.

JULY

If you detest your love life or lover for reasons which are not in your control, then speak up and make yourself heard. You should voice out your concerns before they accumulate and turn ugly. You should make a decision to either end it, resolve it or accept it as it is.

The Scorpio who is seeking love will be spoilt for choices. There are too many options for potential lovers or situations in life, which make deciding impossible. Set your priorities right and make a quick but informed decision.

AUGUST

This month is very good for your love life. I see that you are happy and at peace with your choices. You are in a space where you are happy and feel lucky.

The single Scorpio will have to be patient and continue working on ways to reach their potential partner. You must stay positive and not give up.

SEPTEMBER

Tarot advises you to stay hopeful and continue working on your relationship. Do not give up after having come so far. Problems or issues in love will settle if you stay at it and continue to work.

The Scorpio who is looking for love will meet someone or something from the past that will open a box of happy memories and bring love. You may just meet someone from your old acquaintances whom you never evaluated as a potential partner before.

OCTOBER

You will come across someone, perhaps an ex, from the past. This will rekindle old memories of love and happy times. You may be tempted to slip into this zone, but beware of what lies ahead if you take this route.

The single Scorpio will meet someone exciting and interesting in a family function or a large social gathering.

NOVEMBER

You will get married, engaged or move in with your partner. This is great considering the odds and the journey you have had recently. This month is full of happiness and you must make the most of it.

The Scorpio who is looking for love will meet a headstrong and dominating character. This person is very well read and clear with his or her ideas of a partner. While you do stand a good chance, ensure you know how to deal with such a character.

DECEMBER

This month is characterized by conflicts, insecurities and apprehensions revolving your relationship. You are spending sleepless nights worried about the outcome but most of these worries are only in your head. It's best to speak up and discuss it with your partner to get to the bottom what is bothering you so much.

The single Scorpio must learn to let go and move on. If you are stuck in old patterns and ways of finding love, then let these redundant ideas go, they are not helping you. Move on in life and look at the beautiful present, which is a fulfilling and promising moment.

HEALTH PREDICTIONS

JANUARY

If you are holding onto painful emotions or memories, you must let them go at once. These negative emotions are wreaking havoc in your health and are responsible for chronic ailments. It is good to forgive and, more importantly, forget. Why would you want to inflict pain on yourself? The month ends well where you are seen spending some quality time with loved ones and making up for lost time.

FEBRUARY

Your health looks good this month. You are at your happiest and enjoying the goodness of life. You may start a new regime or health routine that promises good results, provided you stay at it.

MARCH

You are stressed about work and things in general. This stress is overwhelming and causing a great deal of health problems. First and foremost, take up only as much work as you can deliver and stop worrying about it. Plan your life and set your priorities in order. You may have to put an end to something that isn't working out. This will only add to your emotional burden and increase your stress levels.

APRIL

If you are overdoing anything such as worry, stress, or work, put an end to it. This approach isn't helping you at all, in fact, it is impairing your health. You must learn to take it easy and focus on gradually achieving health results. A new beginning shall take place this month. This could be a new treatment, a course or some health regime class, which is good.

MAY

A big change is about to come and turn your life upside down. This change may end something and lead to a new beginning. A transformation lies beyond this change and you shouldn't resist it. Adapting to this change is going to be a challenge but there is nothing impossible for you, not even achieving conquest over this challenge. A woman will partner with you in achieving better health results.

JUNE

You are holding onto negative emotions and guilt, which may lead to health issues. Learn to let go and move on. Don't hold on to grudges or feelings of resentment, these negative emotions are cancerous. Resolve these emotions. The month ends well with happy times, and good health as you are emotionally stable. You must work on maintaining this state of mind by staying detached and positive.

JULY

You will meet a traditional healer whose approach is primitive yet effective. He will use his old-school ways to make a difference in your health which will definitely yield results. You may also meet a counsellor or spiritualist who will help broaden your perspective towards life. You will feel renewed and revived with this change in perspective, and ready to look at life differently.

AUGUST

Your health will make progress this August but avoid overdoing anything that puts you at a risk and don't adopt a grandiose attitude and do more than needed. Be focused and take small steps to achieve success. A woman will influence your health this month. She is somewhat interfering and headstrong. You must try to limit her intervention.

SEPTEMBER

You must learn to enjoy life and let your hair down. Do not overwork or take unnecessary tension. Avoid pushing yourself too quickly in your desire to achieve instant results. You must balance your life and ensure you are taking rest, watching your diet and exercising when needed. Don't overdo anything or ignore the other elements of health.

OCTOBER

You will witness a big change, this October, that will lead to a transformation. This change ends all your woes regarding health and sets course for positive developments. Do not resist the change like before and go with the flow. Life will take its course and you must trust your instincts.

NOVEMBER

You should learn to forgive and forget. The more you hold onto negative emotions, the more you harm yourself. Also, learn to give more in order to get more. This is the law of nature and problems arise when one goes against the flow. You will meet a healer or a doctor who will be well read and commands respect in his field. He will chalk out a plan to help you achieve the desired outcomes.

DECEMBER

There is a reason to cheer and celebrate this month. You may be involved in festivities or functions like birthday parties, anniversaries or reunions that uplift your spirits and give you a reason to smile. Don't trust people who claim to be healers and professionals without doing a thorough research in their background. Some people may try to fleece you, so it's best to arrive at your decision only after you are completely convinced.

CAREER PREDICTIONS

JANUARY

You will be in a good position at work. You are at a stage where you may be enjoying power, recognition and rewards. In fact there could be a good news coming your way this month. This news is related to better financial growth or a raise.

FEBRUARY

You may feel defeated and discredited from your work. This may cause feelings of loss and rejection. But sometimes lost battles teach a great deal of lessons. You should take it in your stride and move on. Correct your attitude if you are being negative, it may prove to be detrimental in the future. You may initiate a partnership or joint venture by the end of the month.

MARCH

You are making good progress at work and work will be smooth. There is a lot to look forward to, and you are excited and enthusiastic about the forthcoming work assignments. However, avoid mixing business with pleasure and stay away from emotional involvements with other people. Do not get carried away and keep a good distance from office politics.

APRIL

If you have been expecting work-related news, it's likely to get delayed. Be patient and the news will come in due time. Your greatest desire in your career will come truetowards the end of the month. A dream job or opportunity may come through.

MAY

You should consider getting more structured and disciplined in the way you conduct your work. An experienced and authoritative senior man will come to your aid. He might take a liking to you and help you organize work better. The end of month shall bring forth a journey which you could be going on for the first time. You will be involved in something new, different and exciting.

JUNE

A strong and dominating woman's influence is seen in your life this month. Her intervention should be kept minimal and you may have to work your way out in dealing with her diplomatically. Work looks good and you are on your way to the top if you continue to stay focused and dedicated.

JULY

You could be on your way up in your career and this month marks a big comeback. You have done it once again, and it is only because of your will to overcome the biggest difficulties. There is a lot of success ahead of you and you shall soon witness a positive turn of eventsif you stay positive.

AUGUST

You are at the brink of starting something new, causing a great deal of excitement and thrill. You will be churning out some brilliant ideas which can change the face of your career. You will launch a business or start-up of your own or take up a new job. This is something new and challenging, but you must remember you can achieve the greatest successwith the power of belief.

SEPTEMBER

Stay away from gossip or office politics. This is not a good time to get involved in such things. Do not fall for the opposite sex as this fleeting emotional involvement will cause a great deal of misery in the future. You may be going through some challenging times this month; maintaining a low-key profile and a focused mind will help greatly. You may take up a short term contract or get into a partnership-like arrangement.

OCTOBER

You are starting a new vocation or class that will teach you a great deal of skills. This is good considering your thirst to learn more. It's also good to be easy on yourself and take things one at a time. Learn to relax and enjoy life amidst all the new and positive developments.

NOVEMBER

You may be expecting some career-related developments that are likely to get delayed. The opportunity will come when the time is right. The month ends well with emotional stability and happiness. You are at your best place in career this month.

DECEMBER

You shall receive positive news of wealth and finances. This will add to your joy and uplift your spirits. The year ends well, and you will achieve all the goals and targets that were assigned to you. This definitely calls for a pat on the back and much needed rest. You have earned every bit of your success.

WEALTH PREDICTIONS

JANUARY

You will start a partnership or joint venture with an intent to make money. This partnership may mean a collaboration with an individual or an entity that promises short-term gains. Your finances in general would be on an upswing and good news may come shortly.

FEBRUARY

Your finances will be gradually growing. You may just get an opportunity to start something of your own or do something that looks financially promising. You have all it takes to make this venture a big success. An intelligent and sensitive man will help you plan your finances. He may be a family member, a friend or a professional.

MARCH

You are stuck in the past. Don't worry about what went by or how things occurred before; that's history. Pay attention to where you stand today. You might have to take a back seat or compromise in the forthcoming days to manage your financial position. This sacrifice may seem challenging but rewards are in the future if it is done.

APRIL

You will be facing some financial challenges this month. There may not be enough money to meet all your wishes and feelings of lack or difficulty may emerge. You must remember that this is only a phase and it will change in time. Considering the present situation and the scarcity of financial resources, you might have to make a few difficult decisions.

MAY

An articulate and well-read man is going to shape your finances this month. His advice is good but you should also consider your own convictions and, if needed, take a second opinion before committing to him. Money will begin to make its way to you and as the month ends, you will be back on track once again.

JUNE

This is a comfortable month for you. You are happy and looking forward to the good things that money can buy, and the stability that comes with financial security. The rewards of your hard work will culminate in June. You will receive rewards in the form of a raise, incentive or bonus.

JULY

You will be making slow and gradual progress in your finances. You are emotionally happy with the way this month begins and everything seems positive so far. But situations get a little hazy and financial decisions may become difficult as you move further into the month. You must turn to your intuition for guidance during such times. Take a well-informed and well-researched decision if you have to.

AUGUST

You will be stuck in a major financial imbalance where your income does not match your expenses. A correction is needed: you must lower unnecessary expenses and give priority to what is important. Make prudent use of money and save as much as possible for the rainy day. Times are going to be challenging and feelings of lack and scarcity may emerge.

SEPTEMBER

You are giving into your vice of unnecessarily spending money and wasting this valuable resource. Curb this addiction to splurge and watch where and how you use the money. This kind of a frivolous approach towards managing finances will land you in trouble, and again create an imbalance in income and expenses that might be difficult to bridge.

OCTOBER

You must pay close attention to an individual or institution that will come in the form of a financial advisor. This person or institution will help you meet your financial goals and guide you as to how to go about using money. This financial guidance brings about much needed clarity and will help you achieve more from your investments.

NOVEMBER

Times are about to change for good as you will see a positive turn in events. Things begin to move in your favour and lady luck will grace you. You will begin a promising partnership or joint venture with a person or an institution. You should go ahead with it.

DECEMBER

You are spending sleepless nights worried about your finances when such problems don't actually exist. Whatever may be the case, you will figure out a solution and getting worried is definitely not the way to manage this problem. The year ends with feelings of restriction and constraint where you may want to do many things, but your financial position could hold you back. This phase will soon change if you focus on the positives.

Sagittarius – Temperance
22 November–21 December

Like the centaur of your sign, where you are half man and half beast, you have an intrinsic quality of combining two opposites and coming up with a perfect alchemy – hot, passionate, intelligent and driven.

In astrology, your symbol is the bow and arrow. There is also a centaur depicted as the archer ready to release his arrow from the bow, which implies constant action. You are indeed the Sagittarian, always looking to satisfy your insatiable hunger for knowledge and philosophical quest by constantly being on an exploration. In tarot too you are described by an interesting card that describes your mutable quality in wholeness, and emphasizes how skilfully and constantly you work towards achieving your goals and aspirations. You are the Temperance card, a card that stands for tempering, meaning changing, a process of transformation and constant change. You may now ask how this is related to you. It's a good question and I'll be more than happy to explain my theory of 'tempering' for the Temperance in you. Read on to discover yourself in tarot.

The Temperance card has an angel standing in the centre with her wings spread wide and with a halo around her head. It seems to be a female angel descended from heaven. She holds two cups in her hands and some liquid flows from one to the other. Take a closer look, the liquid flows from the lower cup to the higher. She rests one foot on a rock, the other in water and is absorbed in the process of mixing the liquids. Her white robe has a red triangle on the chest. The card's background colour is blue with some amount of greenery around her legs. This card is numbered fourteen. Now let's understand this imagery in simple language. This angel who seems to have descended from heaven is you, God's most beautiful creation. You are assigned a task which can be accomplished only by the angels or the gods. That is why you are depicted as the Temperance angel. You hold two cups: the cups of good and bad, hot and cold, right and wrong. You have the impossible task of mixing or moderating the two opposites and creating a third magical component. Only you can do this. Their flow, from the lower to the higher, explains your journey from the subconscious to the superconscious level of creation. Your one foot is in the water, the spiritual world; while the other is on the rock, the material world. Therefore, you have a deep spiritual side to your personality but are fascinated with material bliss. The red triangle denotes the element that rules you, fire. The blue background represents the sky or the heavenly touch and the yellow-green plantation represents the earth. This implies the synergy of thesis and antithesis, the synergy of opposites. The white robe stands for purity and the number fourteen represents balance, harmony, temperance and prudence. From the above you would have understood your relation to the Temperance card.

As the Temperance angel, your main task is to create alchemy. You are here to moderate, to temper or change two elements by mixing them in the right proportion by trying out several combinations and creating a third element. This is not a simple task and requires patience, prudence and hard work. You have these qualities as the Sagittarian, always on the move and doing new things. This is by far your biggest strength and you are the only one among the personality cards bestowed with this power. A more distinct example of how you mix two impossible and opposite elements in real life would be the way you handle two difficult bosses at a time, a wife and a mother, two different jobs or motherhood and profession. These tasks are as good as mixing fire and water, an impossible mixture, the alchemy of which only you are blessed with the power to perform. In real life, people can be opposites and different and that's when you use your skills to synergize them. This makes you the Temperance angel. According to tarot, the Temperance angel has the will to do the impossible and the confidence that she can achieve the unknown and the unseen. This makes anything possible for the Temperance. Take a brief pause, close your eyes and think of what it was that you balanced and tempered last, and I am certain you will remember at least two events.

You are the fire sign: hot-headed, fiery and aggressive. Like fire, you move fast, arrive at quick conclusions and get into heated arguments easily. You are ambitious, opinionated and want your opinion heard most of the times. Like the fire, you are hospitable, warm, friendly and dependable. Temperance loves harmony and peace and will go all out to keep these elements intact in life. This is the essence of number fourteen on your card. You love your family and will go to any extent to keep them safe, secure and happy. This becomes your prime responsibility.

Temperance is a card of spiritual bliss and knowledge of the higher self; hence, you are bound to feel spiritual at some point in time and would want to renounce everything for this achievement. We will discuss this in detail in the forthcoming chapters. For now, you will be happy to know that you mostly have lasting relationships as you don't mind compromising, and being the more magnanimous person if that's what it takes to make the relationship work. You try different combinations to keep peace in your life. The flip side of your card denotes impatience, conflict, lack of understanding and, most often, domestic strife. If Temperance decides, she can very well be the villain in someone's life. However, for now we focus only on the positives as this book is all about goodness. I want you to take away only the good that you have learnt about yourself today from tarot. Use this understanding to unravel your destiny in 2019.

As Temperance, you have a lot waiting for you in 2019. This book will take you through the future through five different aspects: Monthly predictions, Love, Health, Wealth and Career. I hope this book serves you as a clear guideline to what lies ahead.

MONTHLY PREDICTIONS

JANUARY

The year starts with a bang. You will plan to go on an international holiday or simply explore the world by sea or air. There is prosperity and good news related to childbirth lined up this month. It's a great start as long as you keep an influential and an authoritative man's intervention minimal. He could be family or a senior at work.

FEBRUARY

You may be tempted to give in to your vices but bear in mind the consequences of doing so. You could be attracted to a hypnotic and attractive personality who may not be right for you. I see you getting ready to go on this journey of love but be forewarned of the opposite. If possible, keep your indulgent side in check.

MARCH

You will manifest your greatest wish this March. A deep desire of owning or achieving something comes through and shall bring forth immense happiness. You will decide to take a break to either relax or recuperate.

APRIL

You should act on all those ideas and thoughts that are churning inside your head. These ideas have potential and must be explored. You shall end the month on a good note where news of wealth and good health may come along.

MAY

You will be on the brink of a lot of action at work. There is a strong determination to achieve the desired goals and a senior man shall help you achieve these results. You are full of enthusiasm and excitement which is the perfect way to get going on targets and tasks.

JUNE

You are holding onto wealth so strongly that it is slipping away. You must learn to let go and the best way to do that is to give as much as you can. If you have the tendency to carry baggage, then learn to forgive and forget. There are rewards coming this month. You have earned it.

JULY

You are making slow but steady progress in your career. Your work might take you places, and give you an opportunity to learn and expand your network. You are at a good place in your career but boredom might overwhelm you. You must reinvent your work to make it more thrilling and exciting.

AUGUST

You might start a new vocation, course or class that will add a lot of value to your resume. This is a great start and has a lot of benefits. Wealth and money should also grace you, along with some good things that are about to show up.

SEPTEMBER

You might be at a crossroads where a difficult decision or choice must be made. This choice isn't easy and will take a toll on you. Evaluate the options properly before making the final decision. You may undertake domestic travel which will help you achieve your goals. You should go forth and do what your heart tells you to.

OCTOBER

This month starts with bad news. You may feel dejected, rejected or disappointed. Although it is painful, you will recover quite quickly from this event. The month ends with a diametrically opposite situation where wonderful things begin to unfold, leaving you joyous and surprised.

NOVEMBER

You shall receive news related to your personal or love life. This news shall open the door to a new beginning in love. Do watch out for the stress that comes from work. You may end up with more on your plate than what you can handle. Don't be overwhelmed, and it would be best to delegate work to reduce pressure and stress.

DECEMBER

You will be compelled to undergo a change that isn't quite what you expect. This change will bring about certain compromises which are difficult to make but, if met, shall render great rewards. The year ends with a feeling of regret over the past. Wont it be better to live in the present, which is so much more promising and fulfilling? Think about this.

LOVE PREDICTIONS

Your love predictions are divided into two parts. The first paragraph addresses the love life of the committed Sagittarius while the next discusses that of the single Sagittarius.

JANUARY

The year starts well in matters related to the heart. You will be on the brink of positive developments. Your relationship will be witnessing some happy times as you step into January. In fact, you may decide to do or start something new that restores the love and chemistry in your love life.

The single Sagittarius will have a great deal to look forward to this year. You must stay focused and positive as this year could be the game changer for love.

FEBRUARY

You need to get a little more organized and balanced in life. This attitude will help you balance your love life with work. You may find a senior man's influence quite helpful this February.

If you are seeking love, magic shall happen this February. You are about to meet someone charming and magical this month.

MARCH

You and your partner will celebrate happy events like birthdays, anniversaries or a reunion with pomp and joy. This will add much-needed excitement and thrill in your love life.

The single Sagittarius will be attracted to someone much senior in age. Do not disregard this option because of the prospect's age, instead, give it a fair shot. Who knows what may come of it?

APRIL

You will be in complete control of your love life. You may be doing the right things to help it stay the way it is or even improve it. If work becomes too cumbersome then managing time may become imperative. Do not ignore your partner due to your hectic work hours, which may increase this month.

If you are looking for love, then be patient this month. You could be turning into a sceptic and becoming picky and choosy about your prospects; your expectations may be unreasonable. Take some time off to think clearly about your priorities for love.

MAY

This is a happy month for you where your love life would be at its best. I see you ready to express your feelings openly, and communicate your thoughts and ideas without hesitation.

The single Sagittarius will meet someone authoritative and strong-willed. You should know how to handle such a character, who may also be highly opinionated.

JUNE

You are holding onto negative emotions and thoughts way more than needed. It is important to forgive and forget to make any relationship work. Learn to let go and things between you and your partner will improve.

If you are seeking love, then adopting a more balanced approach in life will help greatly. Manage your time and priorities well to fit love in.

JULY

You would be at a good place in your love life where home renovations or house shifts may be a priority. This may mean a coordinated effort from both of you and it looks like you have got what it takes to make this another smooth month in your love life.

The single Sagittarius will be spoilt for options. You have too many suitors to choose from and this decision is becoming more difficult each day. You should think it through and make an informed decision.

AUGUST

You may consider formalizing your relationship by declaring marriage or getting married. Even conception or childbirth is a possibility this month.

The Sagittarius who is looking for love will meet a knight in shining armour. A charming man or woman will step into your life this month.

SEPTEMBER

There is strong and quick recovery in this month. If you were facing any issues, they will fade away and you will begin to do well. Your love life will witness some happy times in September.

The single Sagittarius will meet someone in a party or at a reunion. Formal and social events will help connect you with your ideal match.

OCTOBER

October poses a challenge. An issue or problem may crop up that will lead to complications and conflicts. There is also a possibility that you may come upon a sudden truth or revelation that will hurt you.

The single Sagittarius will meet someone exciting and dominating at work. This person may be in the capacity of a boss or a senior.

NOVEMBER

You may be juggling two aspects of your life this month. This multitasking may take a toll on your relationship but respite shall come in time.

The Sagittarius who is looking for love will be seen making the right changes and arrangements to initiate a new journey. You are looking in the right direction and it's about time you acted upon it.

DECEMBER

You will meet someone from your past. This person may be an ex-lover. You should know the consequences of developing this relationship. It is best you put it behind you and move on.

The single Sagittarius will find it hard to let go of focus from money and wealth. You are constantly working on this aspect of your life this month, leaving no time for love.

HEALTH PREDICTIONS

JANUARY

You will be starting the year with pomp and joy. I see that you are at your fittest, and this month will yield the fruits of your hard work and toil. You may meet a traditional healer or counsellor who will bring value to your life. This person's guidance or treatments will go a long way in shaping your health this year.

FEBRUARY

You will take a walk down memory lane, which brings about some good and not-so-good nostalgia. As long as you choose to live in the past, you will be ignoring the present. Hence, it is best to let go of your past at the earliest. You need to bring about a change that may lead to a few sacrifices and compromises. This difficult change guarantees good results.

MARCH

You are once again living in the past this month. Feelings of regret and guilt or your constant comparison of the past with the present is putting undue pressure on you, causing health issues. You should let go of this baggage at once. You are becoming a salve to your vices like addiction, substance abuse or some other indulgent behaviour. Watch where you are headed before these habits become worrisome.

APRIL

You are going to feel defeated and tired this month. Situations in health aren't all good. You must take care and watch your eating habits, exercise and other routines that effect your body and mind. You may take a break for hospitalization or to relax. This break is much-needed.

MAY

You are living in the past once again, but this month by focusing on the good things that came out of it. This walk down memory lane will open a gateway of opportunities to do something new and different. This will lead to a lot of excitement and thrill, boosting your spirits.

JUNE

You will manifest your greatest desire this month. This could be a target weight loss or weight gain. It may also be a complete recovery from an ailment that was pulling you down for a while. Times ahead are going to change and this change is for the good. You have a lot to look forward to.

JULY

You will meet a kind and sensitive man this month who shall play an important role in shaping your health. He may be a healer or someone whom you have known. This person may adopt traditional healing methods, and could bring about a spiritualistic perspective to life in you. You should consider getting a little more spiritual because, as you know, most of our health issues are a result of pent-up emotions.

AUGUST

You will feel cheated and hurt this August. Stay away from people who lie in the name of health to siphon away money by giving wrong treatments. Take a second opinion if you must; do not blindly trust people at this juncture. You will have to use your logic and get to the bottom of the problem by giving it a proper scrutiny. Your health may face some difficulties this month and you will have to stay strong through it.

SEPTEMBER

A kind but headstrong woman will help you out this month. She will take matters into her hands and take charge of helping you heal. This will lead to good results and you shall once again be back in the game. During this time, you must consider pampering yourself with retreats and relaxation therapies.

OCTOBER

Your health may not be all good this month. You have to watch your thoughts and not let them attract more negative outcomes. A male doctor, healer or guide is a part of the picture. His intervention is good as long as it is limited. You should know how to manage him before he begins to call the shots for you.

NOVEMBER

You will consider participating in a health challenge where you stand a good chance to win. While there are formidable opponents, you do have what it takes to turn the game around. You will make excellent progress towards the end of the month and will be spending some happy times.

DECEMBER

You are a little confused about your treatment options or life in general may have posed some difficult issues. You should take some time off to think over your options. Do not undergo surgeries or major medical interventions without being a hundred per cent sure this month. Take a second opinion, if needed, and scrutinize the options and advices thoroughly. I see deceit occurring this month. You should be careful about whom you trust and what is suggested to you.

CAREER PREDICTIONS

JANUARY

The year starts with a big change. You will end some part of your career to begin a new avenue. This change may be discomforting initially but will lead to a positive transformation if you go through it patiently. You may feel lost and bored, but the only way to change this is by being proactive and creative. You will have to find ways to make work exciting and challenging. Do not blame the job, instead, work to find a solution.

FEBRUARY

You will be receiving news related to work or a job offer that comes later than you expected. It is going to be a challenging phase where you will have to stay patient. Do not get into a situation where the past seems more attractive than the present. You may begin to have feelings of regret and sadness associated with recent events, but stay calm and focus in the now.

MARCH

You should try to relax and take it easy at work. Take it one step at a time and don't go out too hard. You must try to enjoy the workspace rather than focusing on results and achievements. Don't take work too seriously. Work pressure may be mounting with the amount of work you have taken up. This pressure will take a toll on you if you don't share the burden and delegate it to others.

APRIL

You shall receive good news about a raise or better job opportunities that will come your way soon. You may be in the line to receive rewards or recognition for all the good work you have done so far. These rewards may come in the form of a bonus, incentive or raise.

MAY

There is an imbalance in your work where you are torn between two bosses, two jobs or two aspects of life. This imbalance is causing a grave issue and must be corrected immediately. You might have to try various combinations to see what works best for you in the work scenario. You may eventually choose to follow your heart and end your current work arrangement. This will be a difficult decision but a practical one.

JUNE

You shall receive bad news or a negative revelation may come forth that will create problems in your workplace. You may be asked to leave or you may choose to exit considering the situations. This end will lead to something better as I see you ending the month on a good note. You are seen multitasking or juggling between two options of jobs that will eventually lead to stability.

JULY

You will ally yourself with a very strong and determined woman. She is good at her job and can help you in your tasks. You two will make a good team. You will receive some positive news regarding a new job offer or assignment towards the end of the month.

AUGUST

You are thinking big and many positive ideas are coming up in your mind. If you channelize these ideas well, the fruits it would yield will be incredible. You may receive news or come upon an incident, that makes you feel disappointed and sad not too far in the month. This phase is only temporary and shall change soon.

SEPTEMBER

If you are expecting news of job then, probably, it is going to come late but it will come in due course. You are blocking all the good that could have come to you by living in the past. Pondering over what went by and reflecting over regrets is not going to help you. It is best to live in the moment.

OCTOBER

You are eager to act upon your ideas that you believe will help you create better wealth opportunities. This thought is right and you must act upon them immediately. You may initiate a partnership with the intention to achieve quick results. This partnership is good and will yield positive results.

NOVEMBER

You are on your way to recovery in your career. If there were any issues at work or in business, they are likely to fade away. You will begin to settle down and this will lead to new developments. You are eager, excited and ready to take on the new challenges.

DECEMBER

You may face some issues at work this month. Now is not the time to err, in fact, be on your guard and put your best foot forward. You are being watched for your performance and work. The year ends with happiness and joy. You may undertake international assignments or receive an opportunity to travel abroad through work.

WEALTH PREDICTIONS

JANUARY

The year starts with some good surprises. You shall achieve what you always wanted financially. This sets the wheel of fortune in motion and good times are about to come along. Things that were stuck will begin to move forward and you will do very well financially this month.

FEBRUARY

You will meet a very kind-hearted and sensible man who will help you in your finances. He may be a family member or a well-wisher. You are happy and you are making gradual progress financially.

MARCH

If you are expecting some returns on investments, then they are likely to get delayed. They will come when the time is right. Remain calm and do not get restless. You are impatiently awaiting these results and getting hassled. Stop worrying to avoid further delays.

APRIL

You shall receive good news regarding better job prospects, which indirectly influence your wealth. A woman's intervention is seen which, if not dealt with properly, can become a cause for worry. You must know where to limit her intervention.

MAY

You are holding onto feelings of lack, insecurity and loss. You must let go of these before they start hampering your health and wealth. After all, what you think is what you become. Your work will look good as you have complete clarity and know what must be done to move forward.

JUNE

You shall be victorious this month. There is a lot to look forward to. You are in complete command of your work and will complete all the tasks assigned well. This shall lead to accomplishments and recognition. Towards the end of the month, you will meet someone from the past who will help you connect the dots.

JULY

You are at your best this July. Work looks good and you are in the middle of all the action. While you are enjoying the rewards and recognition, there might be some episodes of discredit or of people disregarding your work. Don't pick fights, this isn't your battle ground. Stay calm and this too shall pass.

AUGUST

You are awaiting a job opportunity, especially one that can take you overseas, and you may just attract such an opportunity this month. Be careful about making hasty decisions and passing wrong judgements. Do not get hasty in making a decision, it is best to weigh your options and make an informed choice.

SEPTEMBER

You will start a new vocation or course that will help you acquire new skills. This will add a lot of value to your resume and help you move forward in your career. At this juncture, you are ideating a lot and one or few of these ideas could be the game changer.

OCTOBER

This month starts with some setbacks. You may hear negative news or a devastating truth may be revealed. What occurs now is beyond your control, and it is important to stay calm and patient. You will end this month juggling two aspects of your career, which initially may prove to be difficult but all will fall into place eventually.

NOVEMBER

You are ready to take up new projects and ideate or create some brilliant concepts. You must keep up that spirit. As you progress into the month, feelings of lack and despair take over and you begin to approach work with a pessimistic attitude. You must learn to let go and forget. This way, very little harm will come to you and it will be easier to deal with difficulties.

DECEMBER

You are speculating a lot and are worried about something, which seems to be taking a toll on you. You should take some time off and reflect on the situation that has arisen this month; a solution might just come up. The year ends well with some clarity on what needs to be done and how to go about achieving it. You will be ready to move on to a new assignment or job that could take you abroad.

Capricorn – Devil
22 December–19 January

♑

Of all the zodiacs, you are my favourite sign. The card that describes you in tarot is probably the most misunderstood one. It is a beautiful card: dark, attractive and captivating. No other card has this kind of dark energy associated with it. You are the Devil in tarot. Are you smiling and wondering 'why me'? Yes, you are blessed to be the Devil-God. As you read on, you will realize that you have the power of the demon and the gods. You are dark, attractive and outrageously captivating. There is no escaping you. You are as much in power as the gods. In your card's description, you are half-god and half-beast. So let's begin by trying to understand the Devil tarot card, its physical implications, and its mental and spiritual correlation to you.

Take a few minutes to glance at your card. Look carefully: you may find the Devil's hypnotic eyes overpowering. If not, I am certain my explanation of the card will enchant you. The Devil card has a dark black background. You see Pan – or a satyr – sitting on his throne with his bat-like wings spread wide. Pan is the god of flocks and herds; satyr is associated with drinks and pleasure, half-goat, half-human. He has an inverted pentagram over his head. Look closely at his eyes. They seem hypnotic, don't they? There are two characters, a man and a woman, both naked with their tails on fire. They are shackled but loosely. This card is associated with you on the basis of the traits you exhibit. The Devil implies your dark side – addiction, lust, hunger for power, thirst for wealth and power over the opposite sex.

Devil stands for everything that isn't spiritual, but purely material. The Devil's head is like that of the goat and, as per your zodiac, you are the goat. The Devil's wings are like those of a vampire or a bat, a creature that sucks your blood or life of its vitality just as slavery to any addiction could drain the life out of you. The inverted pentagram is the symbol of dark occultism. The devil's eyes are hypnotic. One look at them and you know you are enslaved; that is his power – of control and authority over another. The two characters denote God's creation – man and woman, Adam and Eve. The shackles around their neck denote their slavery to the Devil but the looseness of the chains implies slavery which comes willingly, a voluntary choice. These creations of God who submit to the Devil have animal-like tails that are on fire, denoting their dark desires and their submission to their overindulgent side – to the Devil.

The Devil card reflects your power and control over others and yourself. You are your own God. You may choose to submit to your desires totally or limit the indulgence to a point where you can seek enjoyment and know when to withdraw. You have the knowledge of the good and the bad. As a Capricorn, you have a thirst to achieve. You will climb the mountain like the relentless goat to reach the top and succeed. This is you – hungry for power, position, fame, wealth and prestige. This card denotes your mastery over yourself and others. This mastery you may apply in matters related to choices regarding self and that to me made in relation to others. On the positive front, if you bring out the devil in you, you will let your hair loose. This is good, considering you work so hard all the time to succeed. It's good to enjoy the dark side of life – sex, power and money. If you can enjoyed these within limits, you have mastered your own self; the moment this indulgent side controls you, you become the Adam or the Eve, turning into animals due to lack of self-control. When in touch with your inner self, the Devil in you can take you places, show you the world and let you win. This is the real meaning of the Devil; it is neither good nor bad but most definitely intriguing. It is all in you; you are your own creator or destroyer.

The Devil is in everyone but only you, among the other zodiacs, have mastery over it. When it comes to others, you can be the

Devil-God by exercising your power and control to help others reach a common good. On the dark side, you may be controlling, over-persuasive and violent in your approach, which can force people to submit to you. You sometimes use your charm for dark reasons especially associated with the opposite sex as you appear physically and mentally endearing. Spiritually, you are the mentor and the student. Since you know both the dark and the good side of the world, your spiritual development rests in your own hands. You can achieve great heights if you wish to as you are the resilient Goat, the powerful and intimidating Devil and a humble servant like Adam and Eve. The element associated with your card is earth – stable, humble and dependable. You are not a dreamer but a real person, grounded and living in the real world. You are practical and analytical, except under the influence of your own desire. The Devil card is numbered fifteen in tarot and six in numerology, the number of attraction, love and passion. No one can escape your endearing charm; just like no one can escape the hypnotic eyes of the devil. You love luxury, adore nature and have an attractive personality. People love you for your character and dependability.

Now that you know the true essence of the Devil, I am certain you are happier to be associated with this card. This is one of my favourite cards and will always be. The Devil card is what largely gives tarot its mystic value.

As the Devil, you have a lot waiting for you in 2019. This book will take you through the future through five different aspects: Monthly predictions, Love, Health, Wealth and Career. I hope this book serves you as a clear guideline to what lies ahead.

MONTHLY PREDICTIONS

JANUARY

The year has begun and tarot advises you to go slow and learn to enjoy life. You may be pushing too hard and putting undue pressure on yourself. This is not needed. Take it easy and embrace each moment. What happened is in the past and you have no control over it. But the present is a gift, embrace it.

FEBRUARY

You will choose to end something that failed bitterly. This could be related to your personal or professional life. You have done your bit but it's time to make some difficult decisions as it may be right to end what is failing to yield. This will be heart-breaking and painful. Staying strong and hopeful are the only remedy in these situations.

MARCH

You will meet someone or something from the past. This coincidence is actually an act of fate and will lead to some interesting breakthroughs. A walk down memory lane will bring back happy moments. You are worried and stressed about something that is causing you sleepless nights. You will have to keep thinking positively and keep negative thoughts at bay.

APRIL

The month starts well. You shall receive wealth and an omen for good health will come. If you have been expecting money, this is the time when it will come through. Happy events like marriage, childbirth, etc., are likely to take place. But emotionally, you seem demotivated and bored. You have a choice to either make your life exciting or stay in a trap of boredom.

MAY

You will undertake extensive domestic air travel for either personal or professional reasons. There is good news around the corner which will keep you feeling motivated and happy. Life will be good and your love life, in particular, would be witnessing some good times. It is good to show gratitude to the Universe for such wonderful blessings.

JUNE

You may feel deceived or cheated this month. Beware for someone may backstab you or try to deceive you. This may take place in either personal or professional space. There is also a possibility of theft. The only way to avoid it is to be vigilant. You need strike a balance and bring discipline into your life. You need to get more organized. A dominant man who is senior to you may guide you this June.

JULY

You will feel loved. There is an element of love and romance in your life which will help you adopt a positive and gentle approach towards your partner. You could also be attracted to someone who is kind and sensitive. However, feelings of restriction and old beliefs will hold you back from achieving your true potential. It is time you broke free and exercised your right to speak up.

AUGUST

You have some thoughts and ideas to generate more wealth. This may be related to work or purely your finances. Act upon these ideas as they truly hold the potential to turn your situation around. You may be speculating over a dilemma that is causing a lot of stress and you feel confused and stuck. Take some time off to patiently think it through and the solution will show up.

SEPTEMBER

You are about to taste success and achieve victory over all odds. This month marks your accomplishments and a major come back in life. You will be doing very well, especially in matters related to health. You could also consider purchasing a new vehicle. I see that you may start a new venture or programme independently that has true potential. You only need to believe to make your dream a success.

OCTOBER

When something ends, it leads to something new. This is exactly what shall occur in your life this month. You will be swept off by a change that shall lead to bigger and better opportunities. Go with the flow and do not resist the change. Your work life will be losing balance as I see you overwhelmed with work pressure and tension. Take on only as much as you can handle.

NOVEMBER

You are giving into your vices too easily. Keep them at bay because they will turn your life upside down. Do not overindulge or overdo anything that can cause a problem. You have come too far to let success fizzle away in a moment. You may be tempted to pass judgements, and jump to wrong conclusions due to haste. Hold on and avoid the temptation as it will eventually harm you.

DECEMBER

You will be ending the year on a good note where you may end up either purchasing a house or moving into a new home. There is also a possibility of marriage or the decision to move in with your partner. Good times are here again as I see the wheel of fortune turning in your favour. Wealth, good health and prosperity are going to grace you as the year ends.

LOVE PREDICTIONS

The following predictions are divided into two parts. The first paragraph shall address the love life of the committed Capricorn and the next will discuss the love life of the single Capricorn.

JANUARY

You will be totally in love with your partner and they with you. There is romance, chemistry and passion between the two of you. This is a great start to the year, and you should use this time as an opportunity to openly share your feelings and emotions with your partner.

The single Capricorn will have some success in finding a lover. You are going to meet someone special this month.

FEBRUARY

You will receive positive news this month which shall rub off on your life and keep it moving strong and stable. A young man shall play an important role in influencing your love life.

The Capricorn who is seeking love may face disappointment. You may be in for a rejection or something that will leave you sad and disheartened.

MARCH

Your work will be in full swing this month and do remember to make time for love whilst you are busy achieving work targets. A woman, either you, your partner or an external figure, shall play an important role in shaping your relationship.

The Capricorn looking for a lover will be spoilt for choices. There are too many options to choose from and this may cause some confusion.

APRIL

You will be enjoying your relationship and indulge in some pampering and spends. You should consider going to a quiet retreat to spend some quality time together and connect on a spiritual level.

The single Capricorn will be ready to explore love and take a leap. You are ready to work on new ideas to find the perfect partner.

MAY

You shall once again see victory in your relationship. If there were any problems, then May comes as a huge respite. You will win your partner's heart, and there will be absolute love and joy in this relationship.

If you are looking for love, then you must act upon the ideas that you believe will lead you to your ideal partner. Believe in these ideas and work on them.

JUNE

After the smooth sailing months, June may pose a challenge. You may be disappointed and feel rejected by your partner. This will lead to some painful revelations and cause hurt. You must stay strong and learn to put this behind.

The single Capricorn will meet someone young and energetic. This person will bring much needed thrill into your love life.

JULY

You shall receive some good news that will help you re-establish the bond of love between you and your partner. This news may come in the form of better opportunities to generate wealth or improve your health. A young man may be a part of your love scenario.

The Capricorn looking for love will witness some happy times ahead. What you are seeking shall seek you out.

AUGUST

You will complete something that will greatly influence your personal life. This is a much-needed accomplishment, and shall bring happiness and closure. Your life will be going well this month.

The single Capricorn will meet a headstrong woman who is adamant, arrogant and yet charming. You must handle her tactfully before you get lured into something grave.

SEPTEMBER

You are losing the spark in your love life this month. Something is amiss and you seem to be blaming others for this situation. It is advisable to question yourself before you point your finger at others. Try working on ways to revive the missing chemistry and rekindle your love.

The single Capricorn shall meet a charming, smart and determined woman. She is someone whom you can trust and ally yourself with.

OCTOBER

You may choose to move on from your current relationship. It isn't working out and you will especially choose to end it due to a larger goal of yours. You are in pursuit of a passion that demands a complete closure of your relationship or an ongoing association. This decision is painful but needed.

The single Capricorn will recover from all deficits of life and gather courage to make necessary changes in order to pursue love. This is a great start and you should continue working on it.

NOVEMBER

You will be in a competitive spot with your partner where battles will be fought and winning becomes imperative. Conflicts shall arise but they are nothing that you can't handle by managing things gently and assertively.

The Capricorn looking for an ideal match will have to stay positive and hopeful. Situations will turn in your favour and opportunities will show up by adopting a positive approach.

DECEMBER

You have all that is needed to feel blessed and loved. You are at the perfect place in love once again. Continue to give love and count your blessings as the universe has showered the greatest gift onto you – the gift of love.

The single Capricorn will tie the knot or announce marriage this month. You will find the perfect person whom you are soon going to share your life with.

CAREER PREDICTIONS

JANUARY

You should take it easy and resolve to be assertive rather than aggressive in your approach towards work and peers. You may be stepping onto people's toes and making more enemies than friends. An authoritative and senior man will influence your career this month. He is someone who cannot be trifled with and you must manage him diplomatically.

FEBRUARY

You will be at the top of your game in your workplace this February. There is recognition, rewards and work satisfaction in store for you. You will be comfortable in your positon, and enjoy the perks of hard work and power. An unexpected bonus or incentive will come through. You could also be involved in important top rank meetings and committees.

MARCH

You will begin a new assignment, project or venture that will be promising and challenging. This will be different from the usual run-of-the-mill tasks that you do. It has its own set of challenges but thrilling as well. You may be feeling restricted, and held back in your work due to your negative thought pattern and old beliefs. You must break free and adapt to new ways to fit in. Speak up and take up more responsibilities.

APRIL

You will be working on new ideas that can lead to interesting developments if planned well. You are eager to take on more work and this is a good way to start this month. You may be involved in a job that involves travelling. This will lead to better exposure and networking opportunities.

MAY

You are at a point where a decision has to be made. You may be confused as your head wants one choice and your heart the other. Find a middle ground and make a choice to arrive at the right decision. You will accomplish a big goal or task which will add to the feathers in your cap. You have worked hard to get here and deserve a pat on the back.

JUNE

You may have to wait a little longer to get what you deserve. You have been promised something and it is on the way, but may seem to be getting delayed incessantly. This may be a new position, a raise or an opportunity that you have earned. It will come soon but patience is imperative. The wait will be over by the end of the month and you will receive the good news.

JULY

You have reason to celebrate after the positive developments of last month. You will be involved in office parties, general celebrations or reunions. However, the month doesn't end too well. You may choose to end an arrangement due to its failure to perform. This will be a tough decision but it's the best option given the circumstances.

AUGUST

You shall receive a hefty pay cheque, a good raise or a new opportunity that will pave the way for prosperity and success. You will be on the brink of action and enjoying the fruits of your labour. This is the month which could be termed as the month of genie in tarot, implying a time where a wish shall come to pass if made.

SEPTEMBER

Your work will look good this month with success, stability and job satisfaction. You will be enjoying the power and fulfilling the responsibilities that come along with your position. You may consider starting something new of your own. You have all it takes to make this venture successful and only need to believe in it.

OCTOBER

You shall undertake extensive domestic air travel for work this October. Travel will widen your horizons and give you good exposure. You will be making progress in your career this month. If you are looking for a change, it's about to happen. An opportunity may come through and give you an overseas break.

NOVEMBER

You may be at a crossroads where an important decision has to be made. You are confused and the dilemma is serious. Make a well-informed decision and think through the consequences before you make a final choice. You may be juggling two important elements of work by the end of the month.

DECEMBER

You may be tempted to make hasty decisions and jump to conclusions. Wrong judgements may land you in trouble so it's best to take it easy, and stay away from passing judgements on others or your workplace. Your work is going to pose some challenges this December and it is advised to be at your best and avoid erring during such times.

HEALTH PREDICTIONS

JANUARY

There is some stress regarding your career which may add some tension and worries, and increase your stress levels. It is best to adopt a positive attitude to stay in the game.

FEBRUARY

You will start a new course, class, health routine or treatment that will bring a positive change. This is good and should hopefully give you good results. Your fitness levels will look good, and you will be feeling healthier and happier.

MARCH

You may end up making a difficult decision this month like shutting down a routine or ending an association that will leave you sad and emotionally disturbed. This may be the result of hasty decisions or wrong judgements. You must consider moving on before your pent-up emotions take an ugly turn.

APRIL

Your health looks good this month. You will make remarkable progress and be on your way to recovery. This is only due to a strong will to fight. But your tendency to live in the past will cause pain. You should work on getting over your regrets and leave the emotional baggage behind.

MAY

You are losing interest in life and its ways. You should focus on reviving your spirits and do things that help you overcome boredom and break free from monotony. Consider questioning yourself about what you are seeking and what can make a difference. You may end the month with a new initiative that is short-lived but promises good results.

JUNE

Don't expect results too quickly as that is not likely to happen. You must be patient; rewards will come when the time is right. There is a new change in your perspective that will improve your health and help you recover from any existing ailments.

JULY

You are worried and stressed about life, which is causing sleepless nights. Worrying incessantly does not solve problems and will lead to more serious health issues if it is not dealt with immediately. It's best to live in the moment and focus on getting results. You may start a new health routine or class that will greatly improve your health.

AUGUST

You are likely to receive some positive news in matters of the heart, and this shall lead to happiness and better health. The virtue of patience can make a huge difference if you are working on a specific health goal. Restlessly expecting results will only cause tension. The universe will give you your reward when it is time. Stop worrying about results and focus on the efforts.

SEPTEMBER

You will take up something new in relation to your work, finances or health. This is a good initiative but its success depends completely on having a positive approach, and the belief to make it work. Unfortunately, your health is taking a downturn as emotional upheavals begin to cause issues. You should consider talking to a counsellor or a shrink who can calm you down mentally.

OCTOBER

You must learn to let go and move on. All the negative emotions are weighing you down. The sooner you drop this baggage, the better it will be for your health. You may receive some positive news related to work which shall uplift your spirits.

NOVEMBER

You will have absolute clarity in life and this will bring about much needed calm and peace in health. You will be doing well this month but you must watch your emotional quotient as you may reach a difficult stage where a decision to end an association will once again cause an emotional upheaval. Stay detached to reduce mental stress.

DECEMBER

You will start a new journey with a brand-new initiative in health. This may be a new health routine, therapy or a treatment that is promising and one of its kind. You will end the year on a good note with a will to succeed and fight the odds. You are on the right path and nothing is impossible if you keep working on it.

WEALTH PREDICTIONS

JANUARY

As the year begins, you find yourself with a major imbalance in your finances. Your expenses exceed the income. You are bitterly stuck between two elements of finance- income and expenses. This imbalance needs immediate correction. The best way to do this is by adopting a positive attitude and calm demeanour.

FEBRUARY

You will start some new investments or take up a project that seems promising and has the power to change the fate of your finances. This is good but only achievable if you have a strong belief in what you have taken up. You shall attain absolute clarity on the way forward and the means to shape your finances for good towards the end of the month.

MARCH

You shall receive financial aid from someone who is kind and helpful. This aid may mean a business loan. It shall sort out a lot of your financial issues. However, there is a need to be more logical and practical in your approach towards finance. You can get more from life if you change your perspective and get more serious about savings and spends.

APRIL

You will start something new that will lead to better financial opportunities. This may be a new venture at work, a job, an investment opportunity or something similar. Your career may undergo some dramatic change or would be getting ready for one.

MAY

You are losing the balance in your finances and it would be best to correct it. Keep your expenses in check and avoid unnecessary spends. The month ends well and you will receive rewards for your efforts either at work or as returns on your investments.

JUNE

You will come across a strong-willed and determined man who will help you out in planning your finances better. His guidance is good but apply your own logic to his ideas and take the leap only when convinced. A change is about to come in your life due to the sudden end or termination of an ongoing arrangement. Do not resist this change and know it will all fall into place in the end.

JULY

You will be stressed and worked up due to recent events and this will cause a lot of upheaval in your finances. You must move on and manage life with a positive attitude. Worrying or taking tension won't help. Your finances will be on an upswing as you approach the end of the month.

AUGUST

You have come a long way and by the time you step into August, your finances will be on their way to recovery from all the downfalls they experienced last month. This was only possible because of your strong will to fight back and withstand the ordeals. To avoid a repetition of what occurred, you must give serious thought to balancing your finances, and ensuring there is equilibrium between your expenses and income.

SEPTEMBER

Your work will look good and so will your finances. You are on your way up on the wealth graph, which is good considering recent events. You may either receive financial aid or provide someone with financial help.

OCTOBER

You should take a closer look at your habits and attitude in conducting finances. You must understand that the constant ups and down in your finances are only due to your inconsistent approach in life. You should focus on first your earnings, then savings and finally spending. Any change in this order is likely to lead to a financial catastrophe. As we end this month you once again find yourself in a state of utter chaos where there is less to spend and more to do.

NOVEMBER

You must continue working with diligence and focus. Adopting a positive approach will help you restore balance and attract positive outcomes. You may inherit money from an ancestral property or similar sources towards the end of the month. Income from pure luck or lottery is also a possibility.

DECEMBER

The year ends well and you shall receive a good sum of money unexpectedly. This money will render good rewards if used well. Therefore, it is imperative you plan your finances well. There may be some issues in meeting all your expenses, as we come to the end of the year, but push through and you will recover.

Aquarius – Star
20 January–18 February

♒

As Aquarius, you are kind-hearted and compassionate, a visionary with the tendency to look into the future; hence you forget to live in the moment. In the present, you can be eccentric and unpredictable, and you have mood swings because you are focused on achieving your future humanitarian goals. I have seen my client lose friends and go through difficulties in relationships because he forgets to live in the 'now'. But since you are such a generous and selfless person, and love people, you usually manage to keep your friends and maintain your relationships.

One reason people love you is your intellect and depth of knowledge. I have a name for you, the 'Encyclopaedia of Knowledge', which is exactly what you are. Ultimately, I would describe you as a knowledgeable humanitarian with a pinch of eccentricity and unpredictability, and a visionary who has a vision for the world, but not for your own self.

The card which is associated with you in tarot also primarily depicts the future. This is the single most important link between you, Aquarius, and your card, the star. What a beautiful name for your tarot card! Doesn't it light up your face and bring a gleam to your eyes? This is the effect the star card has on most of my clients when it appears in their readings. The star is a very bright and happy card. You are correctly associated with this card for many reasons which I will explain in detail in the forthcoming chapters.

Your tarot card shows a nude woman at a lake. She has a pot in each hand and seems to be pouring water from one of her pots into the lake; with the other pot, she is watering the soil. She appears deeply engrossed in the activity. The card, which has a blue background, shows stars twinkling in the sky. There are seven white stars encircling a yellow star, which is the largest in size. Each star has eight points. The woman is resting her right foot in the water while her left knee is resting on the ground that she is watering. Behind her, you can see mountains, trees and a plantation.

The woman is the female angel who represents Aquarius, in other words you. You are the pure soul whose purpose is to maintain harmony. The woman's nudity symbolizes your innocence and oneness with creation. You do not consider yourself separate from the world or its entities. The lake represents your super-consciousness. The pot from which the angel pours water into the lake denotes your spiritual acts; you pour knowledge and wisdom in your pool of super-consciousness for discovery and self-growth.

The pot that pours water into the soil symbolizes your acts of kindness unto others to establish harmony between two worlds, the spiritual and the material; basically, it indicates all of your humanitarian work. The seven stars denote the seven chakras – your aura. The star card is numbered seventeen; eight in numerology which is depicted by the eight points of the stars. Eight in tarot stands for strength which implies inner strength to heal the world and overcome all odds.

As Aquarius, you are the water-bearer, someone who gives to others first and then gives to the self. You have embraced the humanitarian cause of providing wisdom, kindness and love to the world. This is your link with the star card. In star too, the angel is the water-bearer, who learns and then imparts her knowledge to the world. You are the foresighted water-bearer. The large yellow star represents a hopeful future, its light glowing and cutting through the darkness, giving the darkness a bluish gleam of hope. This is why you are future-minded, a visionary. You are noble, practical and precise.

You believe in tomorrow and you live in the future. You are the most hopeful of the zodiac signs. If you follow the star you will reach your destination, not today or tomorrow, but in the future, which is why this a future-oriented card. When this card appears in a reading, it promises hope, a possibility that your dreams and aspirations will be fulfilled. Living and loving in the future is the Aquarian style.

The only flaw I see in this card is its uncertainty with respect to how distant the future seems – a year, five, ten, twenty years? Herein lies a problem with you as Aquarius – you are eccentric, unpredictable and unreliable. Your aloofness makes it difficult to depend on you for emotional support, and this drives away emotional privacy. Your friends and companions are likely to find it difficult to relate to you on an emotional level. You can be a charmer one moment and totally unpredictable the very next.

The star card is about new ideas, creations and distant hope. You are highly creative and driven by remarkable comprehension skills which evoke brilliant concepts. This makes you an asset in your professional field. Your spark can also be attributed to your element, air, which represents brilliance in communication and thoughts. You are clear in your thinking and excellent with creative concepts, most often abstract ones. Air is also associated with humane causes. You are cooperative and helpful by nature, and try to understand the perspective of others. This makes you my star zodiac.

You have a keen sense of intuition as well. Your sixth sense is strong and, if developed, can take you a long way in knowing the unknown. You must consider harnessing your intuitive skills. On a spiritual level, you are very close to attaining enlightenment. Your purpose is self-realization and, unknowingly, you are already on this path. Now that you know this, I especially recommend that you focus on your spiritual self.

You have a lot waiting for you in 2019. This book will take you through different aspects of life such as 'Love', 'Health', 'Wealth', 'Career' and also the monthly predictions. Hope this book provides you with clear guidelines to what lies ahead.

MONTHLY PREDICTIONS

JANUARY

You will start the year with some minor issues especially at work where the pressure would be mounting and you will be under constant vigilance. This is the time when you should excel in work and leave very little room for error. If you are stuck in a legal battle, then your victory this month is certain.

FEBRUARY

You have everything needed to make life happy especially a family which is loving and supportive. You should take some time off to thank the universe for the greatest gift of love. Apparently, you might face a defeat or feel rather low at work front where people may generally disregard your work and may also steal your credit.

MARCH

You will make gradual progress at work where there are opportunities to network and get noticed. You could also receive a good news as the times ahead are about to change. Wealth, health and luck are all about to favour you this month.

APRIL

You shall achieve conquest over odds and come out victorious. There is much to be proud off and you truly deserve a pat on the back for the job well done. You may also consider purchasing an automobile this April. However, do look out for a strong and an articulate man whose interference would be rather annoying. His influence is good if you know where to limit it.

MAY

You will undertake overseas travel for work or leisure. This is a happy month where you are excited and eager to explore the opportunities life presents to you. You could also undertake domestic air travel extensively and will have constant exciting action to look forward too.

JUNE

You are a little out of balance where various elements of life are pulling you apart. You must learn to balance life by trying various permutations and combinations before they begin to tax you. Two important matters are pulling you in opposite direction. Fix this confusion and pick a side or balance these two elements well before it is too late. If you are looking for a job, then there are good interviews lined up but know there is stiff competition.

JULY

You will be at a crossroad regarding a decision to be made from several choices. It is best to weigh the consequences of your action before you take a leap. Towards the end of the month you will achieve completion of a task which was cumbersome and near impossible. This achievement is like a dream come true and you truly deserve some much-earned rest and appreciation for the same.

AUGUST

You are all set to start something new especially in matters of heart. I see that you are excited and eager to take on new beginnings. There is good news this August. You shall receive rewards for the work done well. These rewards will come in the form of a raise or an incentive.

SEPTEMBER

You are once again at a juncture where an important decision will bother you. You must take some time off and think through well before arriving at a choice from various options. The month apparently ends well where the decision would have been made and from where I see it would be a positive decision.

OCTOBER

You are very happy and eager to start a new beginning. There is something that seems to be promising and exciting. You are eager to start afresh and enjoy every aspect of life to the fullest. There are some positive developments that will take place this month. You may receive some unexpected bonus or money that can help you launch a business.

NOVEMBER

You are in for some rewards and recognition which was long due. All the good that had to come, will culminate this month. Your work is about to undergo some transformation for the good. You are thinking of new ideas and ways that could benefit you and others. Put these ideas into actions and you will be surprised with its true potential

DECEMBER

If you are expecting a news of job or work, then it is about to get delayed. You shall get this but only after a while and not immediately. It is best advised to be patient and calm. There are certain decisions which need to be made in the light of instincts and intuition. Your heart will guide you through the difficulties as you end this year. Do not mix business with pleasure and stay away from fatal attractions.

LOVE PREDICTIONS

These predictions below are divided into parts. The first paragraph shall address the love life of the committed Aquarius and the latter that of single Aquarius.

JANUARY

You and your partner will initiate a new beginning in love. If you two were dating, then a serious commitment like marriage could be initiated, and if you are already married then the two of you shall start something new and exciting in partnership.

The single Aquarius will be involved in formal functions and large events which could be the right place to meet the potential partner.

FEBRUARY

You will be involved in events like birthday parties, reunions or anniversary celebrations that will keep you two happy and excited.

There is a lot to look forward to in this month where there is so much pomp and cheer

The single Aquarius will meet a woman who is commanding, a task master and strong headed too. She is difficult to deal with but once impressed you can go a long way with her.

MARCH

You will be victorious in one of the important assignments mostly related to work which shall rub off positively on your relationship. A good month once again with happiness and joy.

If you are looking for love, then being patient and hopeful will help. Don't lose heart if opportunities in love seem scarce. It will all fall in place when the time is right.

APRIL

To make any relationship work, giving is very important. You must inculcate the habit of unintentional giving and see the miracle that occurs when you give selflessly.

The single Aquarius will be in a dilemma this month where either you have too many suitors to choose from or you could one of the suitors to be chosen from.

MAY

You shall receive a positive news especially in career which shall open a doorway of opportunities. This shall uplift your spirits, and bring about happiness and stability that will be rubbed off on your relationship as well.

If you are looking for love then this month is positive as you shall be involved in large family gatherings or marriage ceremonies which might serve as an opportunity to meet the right prospect.

JUNE

You are ready to fall in love and reinvent your relationship. This is a great way to bring a change in perspective and rekindle the spark in love life. You may initiate some new ways to bring about changes that can help renew your love life.

The single Aquarius will witness a very happy month as something good is about to come along this June.

JULY

You will be in complete control of your love life and together you and your partner will decide to undertake home renovations or such other changes that will help make life more comfortable and enjoyable. This is a joint decision and shall add the much-needed change in the existing set up.

If you are seeking love, then refrain from passing quick judgements and avoid making hasty decisions. You should stay calm and evaluate the options that come by thoroughly.

AUGUST

You will start something new which will bring about thrill and excitement in your life in general. Your love life at such would be going well and with this new challenge, there is only more fun coming along.

The single Aquarius will face some tough times this month. You may end an existing arrangement which you though might have worked. This could be a painful decision.

SEPTEMBER

You shall receive a positive news about wealth which will restore happiness and stability in your life. At such your love life is good if you continue to be emotionally stable and connected with your partner.

The single Aquarius will meet someone much younger in age. This person is articulate, smart and intelligent.

OCTOBER

You will overcome all the deficits in life and this will set the course to new actions. You have achieved conquest only due to the strong inner courage. You must continue to harness the strong will power and follow your dream as your partner will continue to support you and be there with you through it all.

If you are looking for love, then its time you acted upon the ways and ideas churning in your head to attract the right partner. You must make most of these bright ideas as from where I see it, they definitely have potential.

NOVEMBER

You will consider to take a break and make the most of this time. You will plan a short break with your beloved which is a much-deserved holiday that will rejuvenate you two.

The single Aquarius will face some mental blocks I working on this aspect of life. You should overcome your fears, phobias and inhibitions about meeting or attracting someone. It's only a matter of time when good things shall come. Stay positive and ask for help if needed.

DECEMBER

You have to let go of all the stress and enjoy the moment you have now. Take the hand of your beloved and cherish the gift of love and togetherness you both share. Learn to relax and enjoy the small gifts of love, and thank the universe for this wonderful companion you have.

The single Aquarius is focussing way too much on work which leaves you with very little time for love. You need to prioritize life and balance the various aspects to make love happen.

HEALTH PREDICTIONS

JANUARY

While the year usually begins for pomp and cheer, in your case there is a certain imbalance that needs immediate correction. You are stuck between two or more demanding aspects of life which are affecting your health. You must be forewarned about the difficulties that lie ahead which may turn out to be a challenging phase. This month is going to be a bit rocky, and therefore it is advised you take all precautions.

FEBRUARY

Your health would be greatly influenced by a very strong woman. Her interference is good only if you know where to limit it. You must also use your logic and apply reasoning to decisions. On the contrary a very sensible and sensitive man will come to your aid. You should hear him out, as he could guide you through the ailments.

MARCH

You will have to bring about some important changes in your lifestyle. These changes may seem more like sacrifices on your part initially but they will render big rewards in the long run. If weight loss is an objective then curbing food and starting exercise could be one such sacrifice. The month ends well where you will be indulging in all the good things that money can buy.

APRIL

Do not trust people easily who may appear too convincing easily. For all you know one or few of these health practitioners may be fleecing you. It is best to conduct your share of investigation before you make a final decision. You shall receive a positive news as you sign out of this month which will emotionally uplift you.

MAY

You will initiate something new that will help your health greatly. This may be a new treatment, therapy, exercise routine, etc. As you move into the month you will begin to make slow and gradual progress. You must take it easy and perform the new routine in moderation. Avoid overdoing anything.

JUNE

You will be facing some difficulties in health this month. It is always advisable to be safe than sorry. Ensure you are eating well, resting well and exercising as needed. Keep stress a bay and manage lifestyle issues well. Towards the end of the month a major imbalance will cause problems in health. You are torn between two or more aspects of life that are causing issues at a physiological level.

JULY

You will be facing some challenges in July as well but these will be in your capacity to manage. You must stay strong willed and fight the odds bravely as victory is guaranteed. As you end the month you may be at the best of your health and will undertake travel and holidays overseas.

AUGUST

You are likely to feel emotionally low and bored this month. This is mainly because you are choosing to look at life with a pessimistic approach. You should rather consider a positive approach and resolve the internal issues before taking on the external factors. You have a beautiful support system called Family and this is your strength against the odds.

SEPTEMBER

You should take it easy and slow down all that you have been working on. Don't overdo anything and cause an injury. Remember slow and steady always wins the race. You will enjoy the routine if you perform it without any expectations and just for the fun of it. The times are about to change as wealth and health both make way to you.

OCTOBER

You will overcome all the health problems if any or fight the odds and achieve conquest in October. This is the month of victory, accomplishments and joy. You shall witness one or all of these. There is a man playing an important role in matters pertaining to health. You should keep his intervention to minimal.

NOVEMBER

This month once again marks your recovery over the difficulties. You will sail through all the difficulties and make it to the shore of stability and good health. But chronic worrying is evil, and this can cause some insecurities and apprehensions. You shouldn't give into the incessant worrying patterns of the mind. Resort to meditation and mindful living during times of stress.

DECEMBER

You will end the year on the good note as I see the card of genie. This card represents happy times and events which shall seem unexpected and near impossible. You will have to, however, be patient for better results. Do not lose your calm and poise if results get delayed. It will come in due course if you choose to stay patient and work consistently.

CAREER PREDICTIONS

JANUARY

Follow your intuition closely this month as there are certain risky decisions which will need your immediate attention. Do not take any unwarranted risk and play it safe as far as possible. Stay away from fatal attractions at work, and don't mix business with pleasure. The month ends well where you shall be recognized for the work done and for the timely intervention. There could be unexpected bonus coming your way.

FEBRUARY

You will be enjoying the power and good position at your work place. Tasks shall be accomplished and people in general would look up to you. The month once again ends well with a good news coming along. Also do keep in mind to take it easy sometimes and enjoy what you are doing.

MARCH

You will start a new course or vocation that will help you unlearn and learn new skills. This is a great way to establish yourself in the market. This new initiative will set the course for better prospects, as I see positive events taking shape in your career.

APRIL

You shall reach a point where an important decision rests on your shoulders. But making the decision will be the cause of concern.

You will be confused and troubled about what must be done and therefore it is best to take some time off to think through before jumping to conclusions. The month will end with some tensions revolving around your work.

MAY

Don't be in a haste to take decision or draw judgements. This might not be the time to do so. Instead stay calm and evaluate your options. A woman, someone strong headed and determined will play an important role this month. She is someone who can't be stifled with and therefore you should handle her diplomatically.

JUNE

Your work will look very good this month. You are at the top of the game enjoying power and position. Rewards and recognition both will come along. There is a big change which will occur towards the end of the month. You may either decide to move on or end your association with the existing project only to lead into a better opportunity.

JULY

Your victory is certain this month. If you faced difficulties at work, then it is all going to soon settle down. You will achieve your targets and accomplish the goals assigned. Once again be careful about a male boss or senior who may be quick in passing wrongful judgements about you and your work. Try and handle this person assertively and not aggressively.

AUGUST

You will be on your way towards some happy times this month as you may undertake overseas travel for work or be sent out on an overseas project. This break will give you the platform needed to establish yourself. Apparently look out for the end of the month as situations get difficult since you could be stuck between two aspects of work which are pulling you in two different directions. Try to sort the imbalance immediately.

SEPTEMBER

You will initiate a new partnership or a venture with someone who promises good results and from where I see it, it indeed looks promising. This venture shall set the course for new beginnings which will bring about progress and job satisfaction.

OCTOBER

You may feel sad and dejected with the way work has turned out this month. While others may walk away with rewards and recognition, you may feel saddened with negative outcomes. However, this situation is temporary as all of it will change if you are willing to give yourself and the work place some time

NOVEMBER

You will busy in office gatherings and reunions. This is the month of celebration and joy. Go forth and make the most of it! The month ends with the onset of new and exciting beginning. This is something that you have never done before and this kind of work has its own share of risks and rewards, something that you will deeply cherish.

DECEMBER

The new developments of the last month cause you to accept a few compromises and adapt to unexpected changes which might not go down too well. You will have to walk the tight rope for a while before you see success. This difficulty might lead to a decision to either end the present association or relocate in order to follow your true calling.

WEALTH PREDICTIONS

JANUARY

The year starts with feelings of restraint and negativity. You are not comfortable with your finances and although you wish to do more, your financial position may not permit you to do so. This will cause some feelings of discomfort and constraint. But if you apply your logic to it and think through ways to meet your expenses with the limited resources you own, then there is definitely scope for improvement.

FEBRUARY

You may be living in the past this month as feeling of regret and guilt take over. But you must focus on what you are doing and where you are now. That is what finally matters! The month apparently ends with conquest and victory. You shall achieve what you had set out to in finances.

MARCH

You must learn to let your hair down and relax a bit. Take life and work a bit easily, and enjoy what you are doing rather than simply doing it. If you begin to lose interest and feel bored then only you hold the key to rekindle the excitement and passion in work. Don't look at your finances with a negative approach, in fact adopt a positive outlook towards it and see the change it leads to.

APRIL

Go slow and watch where you are headed with your financial decisions. It is best to adopt a thorough scrutiny of what you intend to take up. If you are stuck between two options or two aspects of wealth, then this may be just the time to keep one and let go of the other. Try and match your income with expenses which may be crucial this month.

MAY

You will achieve success in what you are doing and the returns will be good too. You may purchase a new automobile or such other extensive investments are likely this month. You are generally happy and excited about the way situations have spanned out and this shall keep you going.

JUNE

You are once again trying to adopt a negative approach towards your finances. It is best to look at the glass as half-full than half-empty. Think about this before you make any wrong judgements about your position and land into trouble.

JULY

You could be stuck between two kinds or financial resources that are eating into your wealth. You must try and sort this imbalance by choosing to keep one and let go of the other. A woman will try and help you out here but once again it is best to use your logic as well, and not blindly follow people's guidance.

AUGUST

You could be facing some serious problems in managing your incomes with expenses. Use the resources prudently. As you progress into the month, situations will get better, and you will once again get back in control of your finances.

SEPTEMBER

You shall reach a point in your finances where two different aspects are pulling you in two directions. Making a decision would be difficult as your head is on one side and the heart on the other. You shall therefore end the month juggling between these two financial avenues.

OCTOBER

You will choose to end one of the above two avenues which was failing to yield returns. You may have done your best but I believe this decision to end was a good thought. Although painful, the judgement had to be passed. You will receive news which may not be all that you expected as you come to the end of the month.

NOVEMBER

This month is good considering all the difficulties you experienced before. You shall be enjoying the best that money can buy and will be seen indulging in abundance of wealth and prosperity. You are rather happy and content with the way life has turned out and this is a good way to come to the end of the year.

DECEMBER

As you approach the end of the year, certain situations may not go as planned and you could face a defeat or may have to take a beating in finances. This shall leave you feeling dejected. But the year ends with a pleasant surprise as something reaches its finals stage of completion and thereby yields the much-deserved rewards.

Pisces – Moon
19 February–20 March

♓

I will be honest with you, Pisces is a difficult zodiac sign to write about. That's because the way I see you is quite different from the way the world sees you. I perceive you as compassionate, gentle, loving, and, in fact, one of the most forgiving of all the signs. However, the world sees you as insane, selfish, overbearing and menacing. You are two people in one like your sign which represents two fish. You are a mix of good and bad, right and wrong, the pretty and the ugly. Only you have the power to choose what you want to be at any given moment.

It is difficult to describe you in a single chapter. You are multifaceted and can be mysterious and intriguing at the same time. It is not easy to fathom you and your sentiments. According to the zodiac, you are a fish, which implies a gentle, fuzzy character. You are not one but two fish, and this duality links you to the Moon in tarot, known for its dark energy and mysticism. It is the card which represents the other world. The two fish represent the two extreme sides of your nature – either too good to be true or too horrible to accept.

The Moon card symbolizes darkness with a gleam of silver light that emanates from it. This light is what keeps you awake and aware of both your dark and light side in tarot. You are an artist or a total maniac, depending on how you accept this gleam of light and what path you choose to walk in the darkness. In my opinion, you are the most interesting card in the Rider-Waite tarot deck. It will be a delight to take you through the various elements which link you with the Moon card.

In the Moon tarot card, the central image is of the sun which seems to be overpowered by the moon, as though the moon is casting its shadow on the sun. There are two pillars on either side of the card with water flowing between them. Two creatures, a dog on the left and a fox on the right, look up at the moon and seem to bark out loud. A crayfish emerges from the lake at the bottom of the card. It's half inside the water and half out of it. The patch of land where the dog and the fox stand shows yellowish vegetation. The card is numbered eighteen.

Let's understand what the card represents in relation to you. The bluish background depicts your ever-changing moods. You are happy sometimes, sad at other times and confused most of the time. The sun, which is overshadowed by the moon, brings out the essence of the card; it implies that your happy and stable mind is overshadowed or overpowered by your negative, dark and confused mind. Sometimes this aspect overpowers the sensible you; that's when the Moon's correlation with you comes into being. This is the normal tendency in a Piscean, to slip in and out of extreme moods.

Of the two creatures depicted on the card, the dog represents the faithful, compassionate, artistic, genius and lovable side of the conscious mind; and the fox represents the dark, unhappy, fearful, confused and mentally disturbed side. The yellowish vegetation signifies the earth, a subtle representation of the material world. The pool or the lake represents the subconscious mind, the crayfish emerging from it symbolizes the conscious awareness that gradually unfolds and the power of intuition that you have acquired from the pool of subconscious which will help you connect with the larger spiritual purpose of your life. With time, the depth of your inner being will unfold. This is where your deep spiritual side comes into play.

If you closely observe the crayfish in the card, you will notice that it seems to have two parts – one inside the water and the other outside it, like the two fish of your zodiac symbol. This represents the opposing elements of your personality, the light and the dark. The water flowing between the pillars denotes your journey into the super consciousness. Note how the moonlight shines dimly while you are on the path of self-discovery, producing darkness and fear on this holy path. If you succeed in this journey and cross over to the other side of the pillars, you will be back into the brightness of the sun, the land of light.

This card is numbered eighteen and denotes emotions, secrets, lies, selfishness, criminal-mindedness, intuition, destruction and mental sickness. When the number eighteen is reduced to a single number, it becomes nine. Nine symbolizes completion, patience, harmony and meditation. In the ancient Egyptian and Greek cultures, nine was considered a sacred number. Therefore, you are a mix of eighteen and nine, the dark and the sacred. On one hand, you are a crazily self-obsessed, intuitive and emotional person, on the other hand, you are a harmonious, loving, forgiving and spiritual guide.

I hope I have been successful in conveying the true essence of the Moon card to you. When this card appears in a client's reading, I warn the person of a difficult period ahead when emotions will prevail over analytical and pragmatic thinking. The Moon refers to the illusionary land where you, the Pisces, live. You build castles in the air and inhabit an illusionary world where wonderful things happen. This is the place where the genius, artist, poet, actor, murderer, drug addict or psychopath in you emerges.

The Moon is the world where good meets the dark. This is the stage when you have to make a choice between your dark and light sides. You may choose to live in the dark or sail through your subconscious pool to the other side. You may choose to live in the underworld but escape to a dream land with fantasies and illusions from time to time. Alternatively, you may stay in this fantasy world, and use your skills and talents in the real world. You can choose to live in the dark and become a dark person or use this dark world to your advantage and make the most of your positive qualities. This is you, the Moon, the Piscean; a thin line of sanity separates you from your alluring, seductive dark side.

You are a very forgiving person, someone who loves peace and harmony. You are a loyal lover, an understanding spouse, a caring and patient parent and an artistic worker. On the flip side, you can be an overbearing, confused and menacing lover. As a parent, you might not be the ideal role model due to your addictive tendency and your tendency to be overly protective about your child. As a worker, if you fail to develop your intellect or artistic qualities, you may end up being an average performer who is unable to understand corporate politics or the fast-paced business.

You are the water element. This implies you are emotional and sensitive, qualities that make you a people person. You have a deep understanding of human nature, and are compassionate and kind. Your most impressive quality is your forgiveness. You don't hold grudges and, therefore, you can forgive and forget. You hold a special place in my heart, my dear Moon, for your compassion and loving kindness. I only wish that the year ahead is as good as you are.

As the Moon, you have a lot waiting for you in 2019. This book will take you through five different aspects of your life: Monthly predictions, Love, Health, Wealth and Career. I hope this book provides you with clear guidelines to what lies ahead.

MONTHLY PREDICTIONS

JANUARY

The year starts well for the artistic Moon. January is a great month for you as I see you happy and renewed. In fact, this month is called the month of genie: if you make a wish, it shall come true. You will be juggling two important aspects of your life in the last few days of the month. Multitasking is the key to success at such trying times.

FEBRUARY

You must follow your intuition. If it is guiding you to someplace or to something, then go with the flow. What lies ahead is a risky period and you should follow your instincts as they will guide you to safety. A woman will play an important role in your life this month. The month ends with wealth and good news coming your way. You may walk away with a hefty bonus or consider using your wealth and ideas to start a business of your own.

MARCH

You will be completely involved in your work, where you are enjoying the power and responsibilities that come along with the tasks assigned to you. A senior man is likely to take positive interest in your work. Times ahead are about to change as I see the wheel of fortune turning in your favour. You are about to witness some good times.

APRIL

You will receive good news this month. This news is like a double-edged sword. It is related to your career and shall set the course for new beginnings in matters related to work and wealth. You are going to receive a job offer or some news about work.

MAY

This month is about a partnership between you and another person. This partnership is mostly in matters of the heart, indicating a love affair, infatuation or commitment. You are ready to explore love and give your best to this new beginning.

JUNE

An arrangement shall fail and you may have to call it off. This could be related to love or work, prompting the end of a relationship or relocation. This was meant to be and it is time to move on. As we approach the end of the month, you shall either receive financial aid from someone senior or provide it to someone else.

JULY

You will commence an adventurous, exciting and unknown journey. You are starting a new venture which is unexplored and seems intriguing. It has its risks but also promises a lot of thrill and excitement. This venture could be a new business, work or some other initiative where your skills are predominantly involved.

AUGUST

You are at your happiest in a family set-up, and there is joy and stability in store for you this month. You can't ask for more and this is the perfect time to thank the universe for the wonderful gift of meaningful relationships. This may be the time where wealth flows in full throttle and important happy events like marriages, childbirth, etc. take place.

SEPTEMBER

You will have to be strong as a relationship or association will come to an end due to future prospects. The month will end beautifully with the onset of wealth and good health. You have a lot to look forward to if you choose to move on.

OCTOBER

You will be actively involved in your career with the responsibilities assigned to you. You will achieve your targets and will be delegating work exceptionally well to ensure your team succeeds. Situations are only going to get better form here, especially in matters of wealth and finances. You are going to witness an upswing in cash flow.

NOVEMBER

If you were facing deficits in any aspect of your life such as health, wealth, career or love then it's all about to get better. You are on a path to recovery and are likely to spring back in action. You will be developing new ideas, and ways to make life easy for yourself and others. You must act upon them as I see a lot of potential there.

DECEMBER

You will come upon someone or something from the past that will influence your future. This chance meeting will bring back a lot of pleasant memories. As you reach the end of the year, you will receive good news regarding better prospects in wealth and health.

LOVE PREDICTIONS

This chapter is divided into two parts. The first paragraph will address the love life of the committed Pisces and the next will discuss the Pisces who are single.

JANUARY

The year starts off with some issues and communication problems. You will have conflict with your partner and are likely to feel defeated. Your point of view may go unheard and this may cause some issues but using aggression isn't advisable, instead, stay calm and let go of this argument. This is not a battle.

The single Pisces is ready to fall in love and will come up with new ideas and thoughts to connect to the right person.

FEBRUARY

The going may get tough but staying hopeful and positive will help. The times are about to change and, if you continue to focus and work on your relationship, it will get smooth and comfortable.

The single Pisces will see some positive improvements in matters of the heart as situations move in the right direction towards a potential lover.

MARCH

The key to success is patience, and being patient in all aspects of life will serve you best. If you are expecting returns or rewards, then getting restless won't help, it would only adversely affect your love life. Stay calm, be patient and you will see good results in short time.

If you are looking for love, then you are about to fall for someone much older and senior in authority. He or she is warm, loving and organized. Don't scrap this option off due to age as giving it a fair shot may turn the game around.

APRIL

Your love life will be looking good this month. You shall attain a certain accomplishment that will positively impact your life and, of course, your relationship. You may consider taking your relationship to the next level of commitment by formalizing it.

The single Pisces will be attracted to someone much younger. This person could be a colleague and will have all the qualities you seek in a lover.

MAY

You may feel disappointed and hurt with recent events in your love life. There are certain problems that are causing disappointment and need immediate intervention. Either you or your partner is causing problems that are hurting the other. You must communicate openly and discuss these issues.

If you are looking for love, then then there is a need to balance your life. You are focusing all your time on work which leaves no room for love.

JUNE

The woman counterpart in your relationship will play a critical role this month. This maybe you or your partner who is in charge of your relationship and, from where I see it, it looks like the ship is in good hands.

The single Pisces will face defeat this month. Situations will not go as planned and leave you feeling dejected and disappointed.

JULY

Your love life will witness some good times this month. There is a sense of equality between the two of you which is very important in a healthy relationship. A mature sense of love and respect will grace your bond this month.

If you are seeking love, then a change is about to set in. A new development will lead to new beginnings and set course for finding true love.

AUGUST

You will be overwhelmed with issues at work and these issues will creep into the bedroom. You will be tensed, stressed and anxious and these negatives will impact your love life. It is best not to mix your personal and professional life. Seek out balance before it begins to adversely impact you.

The single Pisces will witness some happy times this August. You will be enjoying all the good things in life and an opportunity to meet the right person will come along.

SEPTEMBER

A new beginning shall be initiated that will help restore the love and balance in your life. You will be ready to move forward and bring about the changes needed to make love blossom once again.

The Pisces who is seeking love will have lot to look forward to. Do not let time test you and don't lose heart. Good things take time and you shall get to where you want to be soon.

OCTOBER

Your love life will look good this month. There is love, understanding and compatibility in your relationship. You and your partner will communicate more, and bring about some changes needed to make the relationship more stable and rewarding.

The single Pisces will have to let go of old beliefs and attitudes in order to attract a partner. You must adopt new ways to get to where you want to be.

NOVEMBER

There are some issues between the two of you that need immediate resolution. You may have to try various ways to figure out what works best to manage the differences. These conflicts may arise due to the pressure of other problems in life. Work on it patiently and do not lose calm.

The Pisces who is looking for love will start something new in order to seek the one they desire. This is a good effort and you may just come across the ideal candidate.

DECEMBER

You may reach a point, this December, where you are losing interest in love. There is a need to rekindle the spark and passion in your relationship. You must work on reviving these elements and keep boredom away. Try to seek answers within before you point your finger at others.

The single Pisces will have to bring about certain changes, which may mean facing problems for a while in order to make love happen. Certain compromises in life will work wonders in the future.

HEALTH PREDICTIONS

JANUARY

You will start the year on a good note. I see you making gradual progress in your health. You will undertake activities that will help you move forward and work out more effectively. Doing what is needed in limits will help; do not overdo it and cause an injury. The month ends with a definite victory. You will overcome the problems faced so far and achieve conquest over your health woes.

FEBRUARY

You will meet a traditional healer or a doctor who uses old ways of treatment. This healer may also come to you in the form of a counsellor or therapist who will guide you on an emotional or spiritual plane. This is a good way to overcome all the negative emotions you have accumulated inside. You must learn to let go before these emotions of guilt, remorse, anger, hatred or resentment branch out in the form of serious ailments.

MARCH

You are about to start a new initiative. This is an adventure of a lifetime and you are undertaking something like this for the first time. It is a step towards better health and improved fitness levels, and is going to render positive results, provided you are willing to take risks. Your fears and apprehensions may cause havoc. Don't give in to these mind games and keep negative feelings at bay.

APRIL

You are involved in two things that are dividing you and creating an imbalance in your life. Choose sides and move on. You can't be involved in two opposing aspects when you know you only have the energy to deal with one. There is a break coming up this month. You may be on this break for leisure or due to a short hospitalization, which will give your body the much-needed rest for rejuvenation. There is nothing serious, so don't worry about this. Just focus on enjoying the break.

MAY

You will be doing much better in health and a lot of good that will come forth this May. You deserve total credit for all the hard work you've put in. You will start something new like a health routine, therapy or initiative which is short-lived and promises good results.

JUNE

An authoritative and adamant man plays an important role in shaping your health this June. He is a little difficult to deal with and you may have to simply go with his approach. Your health will look up, and if you continue to put in the effort then results are guaranteed.

JULY

You must fix the imbalance that is creating a lot of stress in your life at this juncture. You are once again involved in two or more aspects that are pulling you in different directions. Try to strike a balance in life by ensuring you work, rest and make time for fun. Do not overdo one aspect and ignore the other. The end of this month is the time for deep introspection, which will help you heal on a spiritual level. Try to give your spiritual development some time and energy.

AUGUST

Pay close attention to your body, it will try to communicate with you in ways which, if they go unnoticed, may turn into something serious. If your body is signalling some pain, issue or problem then you must investigate it. An important male healer will come your way and help you deal with these issues. He is good at his work and will guide you right.

SEPTEMBER

There is a lot of action, thrill and fun this month. You will be moving a lot and working out extensively but whilst you do so, avoid overdoing anything and stay away from fatal injuries. The month ends with feelings of loneliness and minor health issues. If you pay too much attention to all the negative aspects of life then your health will not improve. Therefore, learn to look at the brighter side of life.

OCTOBER

Life will throw many problems at you but what matters most is the hope to fight it out and stay in the game. Tarot advises you to not give up and continue working to achieve the health goals you desire. You shall achieve them as long as you believe and stay hopeful. Try to break free from your self-limiting beliefs and attitudes that hold you back.

NOVEMBER

You are constantly giving into your negative thought patterns. You may be worried and stressed, therefore ending up spending sleepless nights. Avoid these symptoms as the problem doesn't really exist, it's a figment of your imagination. The best way to deal with this mind block is to bring balance into your life. You must correct the imbalance and keep your work, rest, diet and exercise regimes well balanced.

DECEMBER

You will be celebrating your success and be on an emotional high. This is a good time for health as the celebrations will bring happiness. You have a lot to look forward to as we approach the end of the year. In fact, you have truly worked on achieving results and you deserve a celebration for it.

CAREER PREDICTIONS

JANUARY

You must pay close attention to your intuition; this is the time when it will guide you. You might be at a stage where decision-making and other important aspects of work seem a bit hazy. Trust your instincts and do as they guide. The month ends with rewards coming in. You will achieve recognition and rewards in the form of a raise or bonus for the work done.

FEBRUARY

Your work will be on an upswing this month. You are moving forward and making good progress. You shall undertake land travel or be assigned jobs where moving to places is part of the profile. Beware of what lies ahead. Testing times are up next where your work will be under scrutiny and questions will be raised on deliverables. You must not leave room for error and put your best foot forward.

MARCH

You will receive good news related to a job offer, assignment or other important and positive matters. The place where you are seems to be restricting your creativity and style of working. You may begin to feel constrained while exercising thoughts and ideas. It's best to speak up when you need to and make yourself heard.

APRIL

You will face a defeat this April which may come from your seniors or peers; they will disregard your work or discredit you entirely. This is wrong but it is not the time to pick fights. Your opportunity will come when the time is right. For now, it's best to stay focused and do your work. A new initiative in the form a job profile, assignment or task awaits you.

MAY

You will reach a crossroads where an important decision must be made. This decision is difficult to make, given the options, and may cause some dilemma. You must weigh your options thoroughly before making a choice. This calls for some quiet time where introspection will give you clarity. Do not let others' ideas influence you and only follow what you feel strongly.

JUNE

You will take a break from work, either for leisure or to think about what needs to be done next. This break will bring forth clarity and a change in perspective that is much-needed. I see that you are ready for a new job and have absolute clarity about what must be done. This can be attributed to the break, which has given you a new perspective. Times ahead are about to change for the good.

JULY

You are living in the past whereas your focus should be in the present. You seem to be regretting something that is causing sadness. Drop it and move on; you have lot to look forward to in the present. If you are looking for a job, then competition is stiff. There are formidable opponents who stand an equally good chance. If you play fairly, the game could be yours!

AUGUST

You will sign a legal contract and get into some other legal arrangement. If you are in charge of the legal department then a difficult litigation shall turn into your favour, the outcome of which is positive. You will liaison with a woman who is a taskmaster and a good ally. You will execute your work well and achieve the assigned targets.

SEPTEMBER

Completion and accomplishment of goals is definite this month. You will accomplish what was assigned to you. This was key in your performance and the returns will be good. I see that rewards and recognition shall come through, and you are going to enjoy a covetous position.

OCTOBER

There is a need to strike balance at work. You are missing out on important leads and not doing what is needed. Correct this imbalance and work shall be streamlined. You may have to work with difficult people or demanding projects and handle situations that are impossible; a balance between these elements can be worked out if you focus. You shall exit the month with the arrival of some good news regarding better job prospects.

NOVEMBER

You may be in a difficult situation at your workplace this month, and be feeling defeated and beaten. Things may have not gone down as planned. You may be tempted to give up but tarot advises you against it. Stay on and situations will improve. You are stuck between two difficult bosses, projects or jobs which is creating a lot of imbalance in your life. You must pick a side and issues will be resolved.

DECEMBER

You have reached a point where you may choose to end what is failing to give results and move on. Doing so may not be easy but it is imperative. After this difficult decision, what lies ahead is victory. You will be relieved that your choice has led to such positive outcomes.

WEALTH PREDICTIONS

JANUARY

The year starts well for the creative and emotional Pisces. You will kick-start the year with good news of wealth, prosperity and good health. Money will make its way to you in a big way. This could be the result of an ancestral property or family income that was long forgotten. This is also the indication of a time where luck will greatly favour you.

FEBRUARY

You may face a small disappointment regarding money. Some expectations will not be met and this may leave you feeling dejected. Times ahead are positive and I see a certain accomplishment coming your way. You will complete something that will lead to better financial prospects.

MARCH

You may buy a new home, shift houses or office space. Wealth or income from work looks good. However, watch out for the end of the month when your money may take a beating. Do not invest in shares or stocks towards the end of March.

APRIL

You are stuck between two options of wealth or finances. You may have invested in two financial avenues, which is creating a lot of burden. You must let go of one and focus on the other. Avoid over-investing or splurging. There is a need to shut down one of these financial avenues due to the loss it is making; you must decide fast.

MAY

Not all your wishes may be accomplished this month. You may have to make a few sacrifices and compromises in order to stabilize your finances. This may mean taking a pay cut or accepting a low-paid assignment for better prospects in the future. You should consider using traditional methods of investments and involve informed individuals like bankers and investment advisors before making big and important financial decisions.

JUNE

This month is a once again good month for your finances. You must believe in the universe and continue to stay hopeful and positive. Ask and it shall be given. You will receive an unexpected windfall of money. The wheel of fortune is turning in your favour unexpectedly.

JULY

A well-read and informed man will play an important role in shaping your finances this month. His experience in money matters will help you gain good results. The month ends with new ideas and thoughts which, if acted upon, can lead to great opportunities to earn more wealth.

AUGUST

You shall make gradual progress in your finances and there is good news coming along this month. It is advised to be cautious about making large financial investments. If you are tempted to make one, then be sure of all the documentation and formalities that go into taking such a leap of faith. Be clear about where you are headed financially.

SEPTEMBER

You should be careful about whom you trust with your money and whom you consult on such matters. You are likely to be robbed, backstabbed or deceived this August, so being forewarned is being forearmed. Be as cautious as possible in trusting people and take care of your precious belongings. The month doesn't end too well as I see you reaching a low financial position.

OCTOBER

You are likely to experience some challenging times financially as you step into September. You are worried and stressed about your financial commitments, which may cause sleepless nights, but worrying will not resolve your issues and it's important you take some corrective measures and work towards them. I see that you will actively choose to work on new ways to establish a sound financial position.

NOVEMBER

You will be overwhelmed by your financial obligations and there won't be enough for all of them. You will have to be prudent about the way you conduct your money. Not everything can be achieved through a limited supply of money and, therefore, you need to prioritize your expenses. If you intend to reinvest in your home in the form renovations and refurbishments, then do not take a big debt as it will become difficult to be repaid.

DECEMBER

A woman will play an important role in shaping your finances. She is headstrong and a bit interfering. You must know where to draw a limit to her intervention. As the year is about to end, a certain revelation or fact is revealed that isn't positive. You may feel disappointed but all you can do is pick up the pieces and start all over again.

Acknowledgements

This book is a product of my hard work, knowledge and dedication to tarot. My mission is to make tarot a household name, and the universe has helped me in every aspect to achieve this. I would like to thank my husband Manoj Nair for his support and my daughter Miara for her patience and love. They have been my pillars and have helped me become what I am today.

Finally, I would like to thank my publisher HarperCollins for giving me this brilliant opportunity to reveal the magic of tarot through this book. One other important person who has helped me with my book is Bidisha Srivastava for the efforts she has put in as an editor and guide. She has worked with me since the time the books were conceived. My books are as much her success as mine. I hope you enjoy unravelling your future through it.

You may also read

Zen Mind, Beginners Mind, by Shunryu Suzuki
An Introduction to Zen Buddhism, by D.T. Suzuki
Zen Doctrine of No Mind, by D.T. Suzuki
Zen: The Quantum Leap From Mind to No Mind, by Osho
Essays in Zen Buddhism, by D.T. Suzuki
Zen Buddhism and Psychoanalysis, by Erich Fromm, D.T Suzuki, Richard De Martino
Mindfulness in Plain English, by Bhante Henepola Gunaratana
You are Here, by Thich Nhat Hanh
The Miracle of Mindfulness, by Thich Nhat Hanh
A Guide to Awareness, by Somdet Phra Nyanasamvara
Being Peace, by Thich Nhat Hanh
Be Free Where You Are, by Thich Nhat Hanh
Intuitive Awareness, by Ajahn Sumedho
The Diamond Sutra, by Osho
Dhamma Discourses on Vipassana Meditation, by Ven. Sayadaw Kundala
Becoming Your Own Therapist & Make Your Mind an Ocean, by Lama Thubten Yeshe
The Art of Living, by Ven. Master Chin Kung
Practical Insight Meditation, by Ven. Mahasi Sayadaw
Taming the Monkey Mind, by Cheng Wei-an
Cutting Through Spiritual Materialism, by Chogyam Trungpa
Lankavatara Sutra (Source – Buddhanet.net)